There's MAGIC
in this
MANIFESTING
JOURNAL

It's Your Imagination

★ Also By Susan Balogh ★

BOOKS
100 Days of Actions & Intentions to Create the Life You Wish For
https://www.amazon.com/dp/B099PZC9T1

Dear Wellbeing: 100 Days on My Path to More Joy. A Self-Discovery Workbook
http://amzn.com/B08PCGR4JD

FREE MINI-WORKSHOP
3 Steps to Wellbeing & Achieving Your Dreams
https://courses.wishmorewellness.com/courses/Mini-Workshop-3-Steps

AUDIO-VIDEO COURSE
12-Week Holistic Healing & Happiness Course

ONLINE SERVICES
1:1 Coaching for Mindset/Happiness/Manifesting
Positive EFT Coaching (Meridian Tapping)
Energy Healing, Guided Meditation
Reiki I & II and Master/Teacher Certification
All or part available by video conference
Set Yourself Free & Be Happy!

★★★

All of the above are available at
http://wishmorewellness.com/services/
Find us on Instagram @Wishmore_Wellness
https://www.instagram.com/wishmore_wellness/
Please join the Wishmore Wellness Facebook Group
https://www.facebook.com/groups/2061444523962316

There's MAGIC
in this
MANIFESTING
JOURNAL

It's Your Imagination

100 Days of Make-Believe to Attract Your Wishes & Dreams

Susan Balogh

This Book Belongs to: _____

Cover Artwork © Josephine Wall
Cover design: Angie Alaya
Interior design: Rachael Cox

ISBN eBook: 978-1-7361677-2-4
ISBN Paperback: 978-1-7361677-3-1

Published by Wishmore Wellness
WishmoreWellness.com
First printing, May 2021
Printed in the United States of America

Wish*More Wellness' mission is to help as many people as possible reconnect with their true nature and powerful ability to heal, to love, and create the life they wish for.

The name WISH*More Wellness is all about how our **W**ords **I**nspire **S**piritual **H**armony & More Wellness...for ourselves and others.

When we take charge of our thoughts in a more positive and purposeful way, we can think and feel our way into any reality we wish to exist in. Living a life with more wellbeing, joy, and abundance is a choice.

Harmony of your mind, body, and spirit is the direct route to healing and happiness.

Let each kind word, thought, and action begin with you and create a better life for you and those around you, one moment at a time. Your positive energy will spread beyond boundaries.

Hello & Welcome to Your 100-Day Manifesting Journal

Humor us. This is a message from your wishes and dreams...

Dear Master Manifester,

What if you could play the role of a person who's received everything they asked for and match up with our energy? When you let us feel like a part of who you are, you can bring us into existence more easily.

How much more can you feel that we're yours?

Imagine being in the qualities and energy of all your desires and bringing them to life. We're in the palm of your hands and you can see us, feel us, taste and touch us. You know that we want you as much as you want us, and feel that we're already yours. It's a certainty that we're coming.

You're so filled with love and appreciation for us and what's to come that you become a magnet for *all* your life's wishes, and we simply *cannot* resist you. Our energies are aligning and we must become one.

So, in case that wasn't clear enough...we're *already* yours to have. But you already know this, don't you?

Perhaps you just need a little more practice letting us feel like a part of you so that we can materialize. Or confidence to know that you're simply attracting us, all on your own with your vibrant energy, and that there's no need to search for us.

We're coming to you with effortless ease, at the perfect time in the best possible way. All you need to do is prepare for our arrival. It could even be tomorrow or next week. Are you ready? Are you ready right now?

That's what you're going to practice doing as you work your way through this journal, as well as lining up with our energy.

And now a word from our sponsor. *Oh, pardon us*. We mean *the Universe*. No disrespect intended. They've been trying to get in a word, so we better step aside now.

Think of everything you do in life as a co-creation and we're in on it *with* you. We're always aware of *all* your desires and taking care of the details. Things are being arranged for you, and answers, insights, and next steps are being carefully placed on your path. Together we have the power to make your life quite magical.

We know you know this. But if you can wholeheartedly trust in it and fully own your abundant and unlimited nature, your life will become more of a synchronistic dance, and an effortless flow of manifestations will inevitably follow.

It's in this state of fearless faith and abundance where you align with every wish, every dream, every plan, every whim. You're in the spirit of it *right now*. And we want to help you stay there more of the time. That's what this journal was designed to do. The idea is to create a more consistent habit that lasts a lifetime.

The intentions, questions, and affirmations in this book are offered to give you practice thinking, feeling, and acting like you already have what you want. We also wanted to give you practice using more of your brilliant mind and creative imagination, as well as seeing yourself as we see you; limitless potential and possibility.

Like an inventor, you're going to put all the components of your desired reality together in your mind first. When you frequently imagine a new story for yourself, it's impressed upon the mind, which then automatically goes to work to find ways to bring your dream to life.

There are a hundred full journal pages with comprehensive prompts relating to all areas of your life, including your work, relationships, big dreams, and everything in between, along with days for self-reflection.

Additionally, there are extra pages of appreciation every ten days, and a few inspiration breaks. There's a "begin your day here" section that offers extra prompts, if desired. And for those, you will need a notebook to write your answers in.

We will warn you now, some of the proposed questions or scenarios may be considered a *bit* of a stretch. One might even say a little cuckoo, cra-cra, or *totally* bizarre, but *we* would say in a good way. And if you find them even *slightly* entertaining, all the better to evoke playful and purposeful answers from you, my dear. Wouldn't it be something if one of them inspired a breakthrough of a lifetime for you?

Can we at least promise this journal will be fun and thought-provoking? Will it elicit invaluable epiphanies? Perhaps even take you on a journey of further self-discovery or ignite desires you quite possibly didn't even know you had?

Well, that is our hope and belief. We'd also love for you to believe in *yourself* and your ability to attract your desires. *Even without doing any of this.* So, if you spend the next hundred days with us, do it for the fun of it. Being in the joy of who you are is all you need to do to live the life of your dreams.

May you always know that you are already *everything* you need to be to go from where you are to where you want to be. If you could see yourself from our point of view, you would see how close you are to aligning with *all* your desires.

Your only assignment is to prepare to receive all that is rightly yours and take action when inspired to do so. Just follow your heart and do what feels good to you. We'll be with you every step of the way.

Are you ready to imagine and feel your way into an even better life for yourself? It's all yours. It's available to you. It's time. You're ready. You have a strong desire for it. You believe in it. You're feeling it. You're energetically aligning with it. It's done.

So without further ado, let's begin, shall we?

Happy manifesting!

Begin Your Day Here...

This is a daily morning routine to further enhance your journaling experience and make for a wonderful day, or can be done in the evening to set expectations for the next day.

If you're open to it, place your hands over the center of your chest, right palm first. This is a great way to connect with your heart and core energy and is said to release the hormone oxytocin which has a very calming and centering effect. Close your eyes and take a few long, *slow* deep breaths. Choose three words that resonate as a feeling of abundance for you, such as: limitless, blissful, and free. Breathing in and out of the nose, think of *one* word on the inbreath, the next on the exhale, and so on, in the same order so you're alternating which word you breathe *in* to.

Continue for as long as it feels good, or let the words fade away. Think of this like training your mind to have a more consistent mindset of abundance that allows you to receive what is yours.

Face your palms down to connect with the earth, and feel its energy come up to meet you as you breathe in. Face them upward and breathe in to connect with the universe. Intend to release any old energy and breathe in pure positive life force energy. Imagine it surrounding your body and filling you with radiant light, and attracting only the most pleasant experiences throughout your day. The power of your intention and belief will work wonders.

Write the answers to these additional journal prompts below in a notebook or say them to yourself or aloud. Follow your intuition and add questions, alter them, or limit it to a few different questions each day.

I'm using my magic wand (my imagination, belief, and expectation) and creating the most amazing day for myself. I can feel any way I wish today and come across the kind of situations I'd like to experience. It's like there's a blank canvas and I'm the artist who gets to design the life of my dreams. A life I love more every day! I enhance what I'll manifest by sending positive energy ahead of me and feeling appreciation for it going perfectly, as I imagined or better.

A magical day is unfolding before me. What splendor will the universe bring me or bring through me today? I am open to receive, and this is how I see it playing out...

My reasons for having a good time or feeling happy today are...

Throughout this day, I am focused on being, having, doing, or feeling...

I'm so thankful for this day being full of...

For anyone I will see today, I think of each individual and at least one thing I admire about them *and* wish for them. The message I am now sending and they are receiving energetically is...

For those I will see at home, my favorite things about you and what I wish for you...

What do I wish for myself? What would be the most satisfying experience or feeling I could have?

★ *I am sending positive energy ahead of me and becoming more mindful about seeing things in a more positive light, including myself. When I create an energy shift in myself, I change the energy around a situation, and the circumstances must change with it. Take notice of any improvement in work or personal relationships in the weeks ahead.*

Thank you for letting all my interactions feel...

The positive people and circumstances and wishes and dreams I am now matching up with and looking forward to are...

How will I look and feel at the end of this incredibly easy day? *Imagine it now.*

I love and appreciate having all of this happen for me, because it will (feel/be/allow me to)...

How much more energy, clarity, or abundant magnetism can I have today? Universe, thank you for showing me evidence of my intentions and how it feels now and in the minutes, hours, and days to follow.

How does it feel when I allow myself to feel magnetic to my desires? I could ask myself this daily to remind me that I am able to align with my heart's desire. I can be anything. I can have anything. I can do anything.

I've made my intentions known for my day, and I am now preparing to receive what I envision for myself, or something better.

Feeling my way into anything I wish to experience in life is all about the quality of my intention. And once I see the results even once, my belief and expectation become stronger. Things are inevitably becoming how I want them to be and believe them to be, in one way or another.

The energy of my desires is like the air I breathe. Mind, body, and spirit, thank you for being in harmony with one another and working with me to create this most wonderful truth for me.

Begin Here if You're Having an Off Day...

By nature, I am in a state of blissful wellbeing and it's time for me to feel good all day, *every* day. And that's what I intend to do. I deserve to feel good.

My mind has the power to create anything I can imagine. And I love knowing I can create the kind of day I want or anything I desire, and I look forward to the results of my intentions in the days or weeks to come.

Since I'm the master of my mind, I'm in charge of how I feel.

How do I want to feel? Write it down or say it out loud, as well as the answers to the following...

What are all the words or short phrases that describe how that would feel?

For anything I am now intending for myself, what do I love about having it?

I *love* being...

I love having...

I love doing...

I love feeling...

I am now shifting my energy to a higher level by thinking of what I choose for myself *now* and in the minutes, hours, and days to follow.

How does it feel when I *allow* myself to feel blissful? How much more harmony can I feel in my body and breath? There's no need to answer. My body and mind will automatically respond to my suggestions, and sometimes instantly. *Close your eyes and ask again.*

I ask myself this throughout my day or anytime I would like to relieve stress or let go of something that's not under my control. Feeling good is more important to me than anything else.

I accept that I am a unique and powerful individual and no matter where I am, who I'm with, or what I'm doing, I am able to stay in a good-feeling place. The more I say it, the more I believe it, and the sooner it becomes true. *And no matter what, it's always okay where I'm at.*

I also decided to attune my energy to the love I deserve to feel. The universe is continually sending it my way and I am receiving it right now. I am a clear and open channel for the universe to flow through me.

With every breath I take, I am more attuned to the harmony, fearless freedom, and limitless abundance of my inner spirit. And something wonderful is happening for me. I can feel it in the air. I can feel it in my heart. I can feel it in my bones.

I am now preparing to receive the many gifts that are on their way to me. I am so very fortunate to be who I am. Thank you!

Daily intentions or questions I'd like to add for my daily, weekly, or monthly goals or desires are...

_____

_____

_____

_____

_____

_____

_____

_____

_____

_____

_____

_____

_____

_____

_____

_____

_____

_____

_____

_____

Day 1 _____

If I could wave my magic wand and have the most magical time over the next hundred days in every area of my life, what would the most pleasurable experience look and feel like?

_____

_____

_____

_____

_____

_____

_____

_____

_____

_____

_____

_____

_____

_____

_____

_____

_____

_____

_____

_____

_____

_____

 The magic of my wand is my imagination, belief, and expectation. I am, forevermore, open to receive the many gifts the universe and my naturally abundant life is offering me. As Albert Einstein once said, "Imagination is everything. It is the preview of life's coming attractions."

Day 2 _____

I am so thankful for the positive experiences I've had in the past twelve months. In relation to my mindset, relationships, and achievements or activities, I feel really good about...

_____

_____

_____

_____

_____

_____

_____

_____

_____

_____

_____

_____

_____

_____

_____

_____

_____

_____

_____

_____

_____

_____

_____

_____

_____

 The more I acknowledge and appreciate any experiences that brought me joy, the more I will invite similar or better experiences into my life. A life of joy is my true success.

I'm writing a memoir book about what happens for me in the next twelve months. What are the names of the twelve chapters and what is the synopsis for each one? *Begin by closing your eyes and imagine going from where you are to where you want to be in one year.*

_____

_____

_____

_____

_____

_____

_____

_____

_____

_____

_____

_____

_____

_____

_____

_____

_____

_____

_____

_____

_____

_____

_____

_____

_____

I am manifesting my ideal year. I look in the mirror every day and think to myself, "I am an irresistible magnet to all my life's wishes!"

Day 4 _____

You have just assumed the permanent identity of the best version of yourself and your authenticity shines more each day; the you that feels right to you, and is for your own happiness. It's not what you "should" be, but who you love being most. It feels like honoring yourself and being true to yourself. Envision yourself in the qualities and characteristics and energy you wish to consistently be in. In the third person, write a story about who you are, beginning with: "He/She is," or "They are…"

_____

_____

_____

_____

_____

_____

_____

_____

_____

_____

_____

_____

_____

_____

_____

_____

_____

_____

_____

_____

_____

I am what I believe I am. Anything I wish to be is something that's already within me. It's all right here beneath my layers. They're all peeling away now to reveal my true power and irresistible magnetism.

Day 5 _____

Write a letter to your significant other, or an ideal partner you are now inviting into your life, or to your deeply satisfying single life. As if they were sitting right in front of you, tell them; 1) What you want the relationship to be like. 2) How you would like them to feel when they're with you. 3) How you would like to feel when you're with them, and 4) What you love and appreciate about them. Don't skip any of these points and add some of your own. Pour your heart out. And then close your eyes and imagine what it looks and feels like. *Dear Partner, Soulmate, or Amazing Single Life...*

_____

_____

_____

_____

_____

_____

_____

_____

_____

_____

_____

_____

_____

_____

_____

_____

_____

_____

_____

_____

_____

Practice this as often as it feels good, and notice the changes you attract in the weeks ahead. *The more I appreciate my favorite part about my partner or soon-to-be partner, the more they show me their best self. As I change how I look at them, my energy and the energy around the situation changes, and therefore I create new outcomes.*

Day 6 _____

What would you absolutely love your home or family life to be like? Your wish has been granted. Tell your family what life is like as you envision it, or tell yourself what an even better home life is like. The sky's the limit. What would you or everyone be doing, saying, or feeling, and how much relief or joy has come with the changes? Dear Home/Family, we are...

_____

_____

_____

_____

_____

_____

_____

_____

_____

_____

_____

_____

_____

_____

_____

_____

_____

_____

_____

_____

_____

_____

_____

_____

 I hold this vision in mind, and as I appreciate what I love most about my family now and send wishes for even more happiness to them each day, I see this picture unfolding as I imagined, or better.

Day 7 _____

I am now preparing for my ideal work life, even better than it is now. Let's say it's happening this week. How am I preparing for it? Do I have at least some of the supplies I will need? How am I feeling and acting? Am I feeling confident and successful, or any qualities that I believe I will have when I'm doing this work I love to do? I am feeling, being, having, or doing...

_____

_____

_____

_____

_____

_____

_____

 I am inspired to take the obvious next step in achieving this desire. As I demonstrate my faith in it showing up for me by doing even one little step to prepare for it, I am letting the universe know I'm ready!

It's time to design the life of my dreams. There's no limit to what I can do. My ideal life can be thought of like a journey on a path that's straight ahead of me and leads to all my desires. I'm *never* off the path. I am painting a picture of my desired end result where I'm surrounded by all my wishes and dreams. What's in it and how does it feel to be in the picture?

_____

_____

_____

_____

_____

_____

_____

_____

_____

_____

_____

_____

_____

_____

_____

_____

_____

_____

_____

_____

_____

_____

_____

_____

It's done. Your ideal work, your ideal relationship, your ideal life, all your wishes and dreams. Close your eyes and think of each desire, one at a time, and imagine breathing in the energy of it or the image that's in your mind's eye. There's no need to seek it, as it will find you. You're simply attracting it.

Day 9 _____

The moment I have a desire, my inner spirit takes on the essence of it, and my mind and body begin to align with it as soon as I allow it to. It's in this place of harmony and oneness with my innate energy where I fully embody the qualities that attract my wishes and dreams. These qualities feel like...

_____

_____

_____

_____

_____

_____

_____

_____

_____

_____

_____

_____

_____

_____

_____

_____

_____

_____

_____

_____

_____

_____

 My faith in my ability to align with this energy is creating an expectation and certainty that I am achieving what I want, or even better than I imagined.

Day 10 _____

My wishes and dreams are coming true. Invisible forces are at work. The universe is at work. The law of attraction is at work. My source is at work. My inner guidance is at work. And I'm staying out of the way by allowing myself to be at ease and have more fun by...

_____
_____
_____
_____
_____
_____
_____
_____
_____
_____
_____
_____
_____
_____
_____
_____
_____
_____
_____
_____
_____
_____
_____
_____
_____
_____

 As I let things feel easy, life becomes easier. Brilliant insights and ideas and manifestations begin to flow.

Fill this page with words of appreciation for anything that makes you feel fortunate to be who you are: What do you see when you look within and look around you in every area of your life?

Abundance

Freedom

Fun

Thank You

Happiness

Wellbeing

Love

 I am exactly where I'm meant to be in my life right now. I am in the right place at the right time and always moving toward a better place. Everything is working out for me!

Now it's time to pick out your million-dollar outfit. What would make you feel like a million? It could be your favorite outfit or newly designed. Let it fit the mood or energy you want to exude. Imagine the pieces laid out in front of you along with accessories. Imagine yourself in it and how it feels when you enter a room. See your face as though it's glowing in the sun. Once you memorize how you look and feel in this outfit, hold that vision of supreme health and wealth, and see glimpses of it throughout your day or week. Write a description of the outfit and then list all the emotions you feel when you're wearing it. And hold that thought.

_____

_____

_____

_____

_____

_____

_____

_____

_____

_____

_____

_____

_____

_____

_____

_____

_____

_____

_____

_____

_____

_____

_____

 You're becoming one with who you truly are; a radiant, magnetic force that attracts your desires with ease and joy.

Now that you have your million dollar outfit picked out, you need to add one more accessory. It's your wealth belt, or you might call it an energy belt. You can name it anything you wish, but everything is energy, and this belt symbolizes your inexhaustible supply of wellbeing or anything you want. It has front and back pockets and each one represents the many different forms of wealth that are available and continually flowing to you from all directions. For example, they could hold your limitless supply of the best health, happiness, love, harmony, opportunities, financial abundance, adventure, inner guidance, and your infinite spiritual energy. You can have it all. Give it a name, color, and texture, and what each pocket represents. Then draw a picture of it and add a favorite symbol to help you remember it. If it makes you laugh to think of it, even better. Being playful and purposeful brings positive outcomes and opportunities to you with effortless ease. Once you're done writing, close your eyes and imagine it being a part of you and your energy. Feel that it's around your waist, and a part of who you are. It's all around you, as all forms of wealth are.

From this point forward, see glimpses of your million dollar wardrobe and feel the energy of wealth around you and how close you are to it. Does it sparkle or shine? Is it lit up in starry lights? Anything to make you feel more radiant, I suppose. It's a part of your energy now. See cash strapped to you if you must, but find a way to feel the energy of this abundant wealth that is yours to have. Your attention to it is calling it to you. And it wants you.

You're worth a million. Actually, you're priceless. And there's no limit to what you can do.

Day 13 _____

What level of enthusiasm do I think the universe has when facilitating the manifestation of my desires? How much of that can I muster so I can line up with that energy? I believe in my desires, and believe it's all happening for me because...

_____

_____

_____

_____

_____

_____

_____

_____

_____

_____

_____

_____

_____

_____

_____

_____

_____

_____

_____

_____

_____

_____

_____

_____

When I fully trust and believe that I am one with my limitless source or universe, I am one with all my wishes and dreams. The same energy that's in my desires is in me and it's bringing us together. How much more abundant can I feel now and in the hours and days ahead?

If my wishes and dreams could speak to me, what do I think they would say? They're telling me what they will do for me, how they will improve my life, and what they want me to do to achieve them. Make a list of goals or dreams on the left and leave space between each one to write the answers.

_____

_____

_____

_____

_____

_____

_____

_____

_____

_____

_____

_____

_____

_____

_____

_____

_____

_____

_____

_____

Now look at each desire one at a time and close your eyes to picture it. It's in front of you and you're breathing in the energy of it. In your second breath, watch it coming toward you. Then feel that you're experiencing it in some way, whether you're touching it, walking inside it, using it, or showing it to someone. Feel the emotion associated with being there. Let a smile form on your face. My life is now transforming to accommodate my every wish.

Day 15 _____

I decided to face any fears I had, and more doors to more fun and success seemed to swing wide open within forty-eight hours. Any time I discovered that I may have a fear of something, I just imagined myself handling it easily and confidently. I'm just practicing the feeling of fearless courage until I make it come naturally to me. What would that look and feel like for me? And what kind of fun and success followed?

_____

_____

_____

_____

_____

_____

_____

_____

_____

_____

_____

_____

_____

_____

_____

_____

_____

_____

_____

_____

_____

_____

_____

 Close your eyes and see yourself doing it right now. I am focused and unstoppable in doing anything I set out to do in my life. All self-doubt has left me, and I feel free.

This is your money talking. We represent more joy and freedom. We represent your limitless choices. Don't be afraid of us. Embrace us. When you seek more abundance and wish it for others, you align with us, as well as the source that created you. Wanting more for yourself and others is part of your true nature and really good for you. List all the ways you delight in seeing others' success and happiness in their life.

_____

_____

_____

_____

_____

_____

_____

_____

_____

_____

_____

_____

_____

_____

_____

_____

_____

_____

_____

_____

_____

I am genuinely happy for others' success and feel that I am naturally achieving success as well. I'll never yearn for it, for I know it's rightly mine. I am happily and continuously receiving my eternal health, wealth, and happiness. The more joy I have, the more successful I am.

I am a superhero and I have one or more superpowers. What are my superpowers and how are they serving me in each area of my life? How is it serving others in my life, or how do I think others feel about how I affect them? How is it serving those who are coming into my life that I expect will find value in what I offer? And most importantly, what does my costume look like, and how do I feel when I'm in it, and using my superpowers? You know, that part of me that is full of supreme confidence and radiant love and joy? I'm awesome! The answers to *all* of these questions are...

_____

_____

_____

_____

_____

_____

_____

_____

_____

_____

_____

_____

_____

_____

_____

_____

_____

_____

_____

_____

_____

_____

I imagine myself in this get-up anytime I desire more confidence or radiance. It's like using my magic wand. I have one of those too, by the way. I use it to grant wishes. When I envision positive outcomes for others from my state of joy and wellbeing, there's potential for change.

There is something you've been wanting to change about your life, and it has now come to pass. There's a feeling of relief that has come with it. What is it and what are you telling your closest friend about it?

_____
_____
_____
_____
_____
_____
_____
_____
_____
_____
_____
_____
_____
_____
_____
_____
_____
_____
_____
_____
_____
_____
_____
_____
_____

They thought they noticed a change in you and responded excitedly to your news. What did they say in response? Close your eyes and imagine it now.

Day 19 _____

Your intuition here; we gave you a random impulse to stop and get some ice cream, and you ended up meeting someone who became a great friend in the weeks to follow. Now they're offering you an opportunity of a lifetime. What could this life-changing question be? Is it business related or personal, and what will you say? How do things turn out and how does it feel? Tell your fairytale.

_____
_____
_____
_____
_____
_____
_____
_____
_____
_____
_____
_____
_____
_____
_____
_____
_____
_____
_____
_____
_____
_____
_____
_____
_____

 When did it start getting so easy for me to listen to these impulses? I wake up every day and feel as if something wonderful is about to happen. Something like this!

I received an anonymous letter in the mail. It tells me more of everything I've ever wanted to hear from the time I was born, as well as the words I'd like to be telling myself and be my natural habit of thought. I love the idea of having this instilled in my mind, and letting it align me with the abundant life I know is mine to have. What does it say?

_____

_____

_____

_____

_____

_____

_____

_____

_____

_____

_____

_____

_____

_____

_____

_____

_____

_____

_____

_____

_____

_____

I love being my own best friend. Loving and accepting myself is creating the loveliest life experiences I could ever imagine. When I value myself, I invite others to do the same. I am now attracting happier and healthier relationships and fun times. I say YES to this!

A WISH Moment for Inspiration
Words Inspire Spiritual Harmony

Dear Wishes & Dreams,

Thank you for inspiring me to be the person I was born to be. Thank you for getting me out of bed every morning feeling excited and ready for my day. Thank you for giving me a reason to look forward to tomorrow and for *all* that is to *be* for me. *Without* you, I might be content. But *with* you, I am deeply satisfied by every moment, knowing I am moving forward in my life with purpose. And every impulse or insight I receive that gives me the knowhow to acquire my desire creates the most magical kind of life I can live. So I thank you for this. And I thank you kindly for finding your way to me. I am an irresistible magnet to each and every one of you. I love and appreciate every aspect of what life can bring me, and thinking of you makes it all so worthwhile.

Dear Universe,

Thank you for keeping me in your sights and continually providing me with wondrous ways to match up with my wishes and dreams. Thank you for always bringing me new ideas and all that I need or want at the perfect time in the most enjoyable ways. Thank you for showing me evidence of my positive thoughts and energy that let me know when I'm going in the right direction. And thank you for the continual flow of wellbeing and abundance that you're sending my way. I love knowing I am able to practice the feeling that allows me to fully receive it, and let anything else fall away. It's just a decision I'm making to stay attuned to the harmony of my inner spirit, to the best of my ability, and every little thing I've been wishing for starts to unfold before me. There's no limit to what I can do because of you.

Dear Mind, Body, and Spirit,

Thank you for being in harmony with one another and joining me in creating the life I choose to live. Each day I remind myself that you are stable and strong and keeping me calm, balanced, and full of joy, and I appreciate you for making that happen for me. Thank you for my clarity and boundless energy and blissful wellbeing *each* and *every* day. Thank you for following my lead and letting go of anything that doesn't serve me. And thank you for keeping all of this in the forefront of the mind and letting it be the only way I know how to be. I love knowing that my mind and body are functioning perfectly and always responding to my direction, and brilliantly so. I am in charge of my life, and I decided to experience more joy, love, wellbeing, and total abundance in any form I wish to have it in. Without limitation. Without self-doubt. And without fear. From this point forward, with a one-pointed focus on a feeling of faith and trust, I am taking myself on an endless journey to way more freedom and fun and self-discovery. My thoughts, intentions, and energy are not only powerful, they are actually certain to create my desired reality when I have not one shred of doubt that they will. I am on a quest to master my manifesting abilities, and so it shall be. I am rock solid and unstoppable, and my ability to attract my desires is becoming effortless for me. So thank you for helping me believe in myself, love and accept myself, and see anything that life brings my way as a potential opportunity for my growth.

This is a wonderful way to energetically connect with your inner guidance or your wishes and dreams. It's like having an imaginary conversation, and before you know it, you're receiving answers and insights or gaining clarity on decisions, solutions, or next steps. And don't be surprised if your days begin to feel orchestrated to accommodate your wishes. To make it even more powerful, consider using a symbol to address your intentions to, even one for every desire. They can be as simple as a crystal, photo, or figurine. Be sure to include one for your inner being. This is a very powerful manifesting tool because you're making the conversation feel real, as far as your mind is concerned. The best part is how your energy will light up. Make it a daily or weekly practice if it feels good, and pay attention to any remarkable changes in your everyday life.

Try it now if you'd like.

Dear _____,

_____

_____

_____

_____

_____

_____

_____

_____

_____

_____

_____

_____

_____

_____

_____

_____

_____

_____

For anything I need or want. I can easily bring it into my experience by appreciating what I am now attracting and receiving.

Fill this page with words of appreciation for all the wellbeing and abundance that's on its way to you, as well as how it makes you feel when you have it.

Abundance

Freedom

Fun

Thank You

Happiness

Wellbeing

Love

 Daydream about all of this flowing into your life as often as you'd like if it feels good.

You were born with a gift. Let's call it a virtual button. You can use it whenever you need it. Thinking of it activates your belief in your natural power to heal, love, or magnetically attract anything you wish. Using the button represents your decision and commitment to a particular mindset, transformation, or state of being you're choosing. And it's done. Ta-da! From this point forward, what will you use your button for?

_____

_____

_____

_____

_____

_____

_____

_____

_____

_____

_____

_____

_____

_____

_____

_____

_____

_____

_____

This belief, this innate ability, this magnetism, this power to decide and accomplish anything you want to be or have or do is inside you. It's a part of you. It never leaves you. We, the source from which you came, never leave your side. When you go about your day, know that all power is working with you and all things are possible. Move forth on this illuminated path and let this awareness be your source of confidence and power in anything you do.

All of your wishes and dreams are literally being delivered to you. They're on their way. They will arrive at your doorstep when you're aligned and ready to receive them. How are you acting and feeling? If they were to show up any day, are you showing the universe that you're ready for them? To be ready for my desires, I am acting as if...

_____

_____

_____

_____

_____

_____

_____

_____

_____

_____

_____

_____

_____

_____

_____

_____

_____

_____

_____

_____

_____

_____

_____

_____

_____

I am who I want to be and I continue to evolve. And my desires feel like a part of me now, and I am a part of them. So much so that there's no other way for my reality to be for me. There's no stopping us now. It's all been arranged.

I realized the only thing that ever made me feel stuck in life was when I was bored or had too much time to overthink things. When I'm doing even one thing that feels purposeful or inspired, it keeps me from getting into that funk. If I find something of interest to look forward to, I suddenly regain my zest for life and even forget about stress or discomfort, if any. I feel full of energy and can't stop thinking about this new thing I'm so excited to be doing or learning. The kinds of things that keep me in the energy of what's to come and interested in life are...

_____

_____

_____

_____

_____

_____

_____

_____

_____

_____

_____

_____

_____

_____

_____

_____

_____

_____

_____

_____

_____

_____

 I feel like life is a gift and something to celebrate every single day! I am allowing my radiant energy to fill me up and spill over into all areas of my life, and into anything I put my heart into. Why am I so fortunate?

You just opened a new home business that incorporates your favorite hobby. It could be something you make and sell or teach others how to do. What equipment are you buying, and what else has to be done to prepare for your first customers? Write the details, and then imagine them walking in the door and add a description of your time together.

_____

_____

_____

_____

_____

_____

_____

_____

_____

_____

_____

_____

_____

_____

_____

_____

_____

_____

_____

_____

_____

_____

_____

 I am playful and purposeful and positive outcomes and opportunities find me. When did my life become so easy and fun?

Each night as I go to sleep I imagine I'm in the life of my dreams. What if I was in a new bed, with the person I chose to have with me, and in the energy of the house and career I desire? How does that feel? As I lie there I take myself through the steps that occur as I wake up, put my feet on the new floor, and prepare for my day. Will there be a new office in my house? A new job to go to? What's for breakfast in what kind of kitchen? What's in the driveway? What do I see in the yard when I look out the window? How does it feel to be there? Like relief, success, overjoyed, peaceful, or limitless? Write out all the details of this vision and how it feels.

_____

_____

_____

_____

_____

_____

_____

_____

_____

_____

_____

_____

_____

_____

_____

_____

_____

_____

_____

_____

_____

Close your eyes and imagine it now, and again each night if it feels good. Remember to reach out and touch something, or see, hear, taste or feel something in each room or place. I am becoming one with the energy of my desire and making it mine. As Thomas Edison once said, "Never go to sleep without a request to your subconscious."

I used to dismiss the nudges to do something if the idea didn't make sense to me at the time. When I realized it could be my intuition speaking, I got better at paying attention to it and it's leading to some surprising life-changing things for me. Just imagine if you put off an impulse to go somewhere or leave earlier or later, and kept missing the perfect time to line up with an opportunity awaiting you? The universe will keep trying, so no worries there, but our awareness of this guidance sure could make life flow a lot easier. When I follow the hunches that feel good to me, what are some examples of my endless possibilities (besides a great parking spot or missing a stressful situation)?

_____
_____
_____
_____
_____
_____
_____
_____
_____
_____
_____
_____
_____
_____
_____
_____
_____
_____
_____
_____
_____
_____
_____

Every choice and every turn I take in life results in something completely different for me. And every person I meet is a potential link to a whole slew of opportunities, gifts, people, or experiences that could change my entire life. It's fantastic!

I woke up one morning with a sudden urge to play the lottery and won the jackpot. Later that day, I remembered that I had written myself a big check a while back and kept it in my wallet. I pulled it out and discovered I had written it for that date for around the same amount. I just did it for the fun of it, but look what happened. The increased number of choices and fun times this brings into my life are...

_____
_____
_____
_____
_____
_____
_____
_____
_____
_____
_____
_____
_____
_____
_____
_____
_____
_____
_____
_____
_____
_____
_____

 Money is just another form of energy and is plentiful, but it has nowhere near the value or power of the loving energy that I'm attracting it with. Love is my attracter for all my wishes and dreams. And the joy in my heart is my success.

One day I decided to write down all the things I wanted to let go: any limiting beliefs, guilt, resentment, self-doubt, or unwanted habits. I acknowledged them and made peace with it in whatever way I felt comfortable, said goodbye to it, and shredded the paper. My intention was to take any time or energy I ever gave to it, if any, and put my full energy into who I am *now*. I decided to have a one-pointed focus to be in harmony with my natural born, pure positive energy. And I felt free. I started using the word harmony any time I started to feel an unwanted thought or memory come up. It let my mind know that I was changing the pattern of thought. This created new neural pathways and past issues were resolved. Taking my attention away from them made them go dormant. Wellbeing and abundance is my active thought and vibration now. The word "harmony" is my new trigger that instantly replaces unwanted thoughts or emotions. I then envision myself on a beach or at my favorite place. The word *I* would choose and its meaning that resonates for me, and the vision of *my* favorite place that I can use for this purpose, if desired, is...

_____

_____

_____

_____

_____

_____

_____

_____

_____

_____

_____

_____

_____

_____

_____

_____

_____

_____

I acknowledge all that was and honor my well-deserved good feeling mind and body with thoughts of wellbeing. How I feel is so important to me that I am easily letting go of anything that doesn't serve me. If desired, write a list, tear it up, and intend to use your word as needed.

It's time for an adventure and a fresh start. I'm taking a break from home and work just to see where life takes me. I'm completely free of all the usual obligations for a year or more, and what I'm doing is not affecting anyone. What will I do? I can live on a sailboat or lay on the beach and read books all day if I want to. Take a train ride or road trip? Or I could be at the airport choosing a one-way ticket. What am I choosing to do, and how would it feel to be away from life as I know it? Imagine it now. Write the details, including what I noticed missing, and what felt easy to leave behind.

_____

_____

_____

_____

_____

_____

_____

_____

_____

_____

_____

_____

_____

_____

_____

_____

_____

_____

_____

_____

_____

_____

I am exploring self-discovery and learning more of what I'm wanting, or perhaps gaining clarity on what's important to me in life. It's all very good. And no matter what I'm doing, or not doing, it's always okay with me. The self-acceptance and ease I find in any situation brings new ideas to light.

Day 30 _____

I love knowing that all I need to do to attract an even better life is to appreciate where I am in whatever way I can. When I have a sincere appreciation for what I've chosen for myself, whether it's a job, a partner, or something else, I'm putting the kind of positive energy into it that paves the way for a better future. So even if I'm not feeling quite fulfilled with something, I focus on the parts I like. And this way, I set myself up for the best possible circumstances in the next experience I have. My favorite things about each area of my life are...

_____

_____

_____

_____

_____

_____

_____

_____

_____

_____

_____

_____

_____

_____

_____

_____

_____

_____

_____

_____

_____

_____

_____

 I am a powerful personality and wherever I arrive, I radiate pure love; the highest, most powerful energy of all.

Fill this page with words of appreciation for everyone in your family or anyone you wish, including those you would like to improve your relationship with.

Abundance

Freedom

Fun

Thank You

Happiness

Wellbeing

Love

 I focus on anything in my life that I feel good about, and more things like it will come.

Day 31 _____

You're in a great big store right now and you have to buy all new furniture and decor for your new home, or perhaps a second home. What are you getting? What are the most inspiring things that bring you joy and will be nice to have around you? Tell us the home's location, everything you're picking out, and what room it will go in. Describe the colors, textures, and more. Don't forget to imagine watching the delivery come, being carried into the house, and trying out the furniture, bed, or tv. How does it look and feel?

_____
_____
_____
_____
_____
_____
_____
_____
_____
_____
_____
_____
_____
_____
_____
_____
_____
_____
_____
_____
_____
_____
_____
_____
_____

 I am mastering my abundance mindset and allowing positive outcomes and opportunities to find me.

You've been given a role in a play that's based on a book that was written about your life. You get to play yourself, of course. This play is primarily based on events that occur in the next five years of your life. Is it an adventure? A romance? Or both? Or something else? Describe this play in detail from a narrator's point of view describing how you, "he," "she," or "they" lived their life and how they felt. Include the setting, costumes, and what big changes were involved.

_____

_____

_____

_____

_____

_____

_____

_____

_____

_____

_____

_____

_____

_____

_____

_____

_____

_____

_____

_____

_____

_____

 My life's vision is clear and the more I believe in it, the more certain I am it's coming true, and the quicker it arrives.

When you were at a friend's party yesterday, you met a new like-minded friend or ideal date. How did it feel to meet them, and what did you say to get the conversation started? What are they like, and what are your plans this weekend?

_____
_____
_____
_____
_____
_____
_____
_____
_____
_____
_____
_____
_____
_____
_____
_____
_____
_____
_____
_____
_____
_____
_____
_____
_____

Every time I meet a new person there's a whole new world of possibilities for me. And even when something doesn't work out, I notice how it leads to more personal growth and that results in more good things.

You've been asked to speak at a global-wide event to share something you believe would help others achieve a healthier, happier, and more abundant life. What do you want the world to know? If you knew it was anonymous, is there something you would add to your speech? What is the response from the audience? Tell us all about it. If desired, choose another topic for your speech.

_____
_____
_____
_____
_____
_____
_____
_____
_____
_____
_____
_____
_____
_____
_____
_____
_____
_____
_____
_____
_____
_____
_____
_____
_____

Close your eyes, repeat your message and feel that you're sending it out, and anyone in your vibrational range is receiving it. Feel the love and wishes coming back to you. The energy within me is pure and present and joyful and spreads beyond boundaries.

A friend of mine planned a nonrefundable, all-inclusive trip with their spouse who is unable to go at the last minute, and I'm asked to join them. It happens to be the exact place I've had on my wish list for years. Where is it, what activities or events do we attend, and how does it feel to be there?

_____

_____

_____

_____

_____

_____

_____

_____

_____

_____

_____

_____

_____

_____

_____

_____

_____

_____

_____

_____

_____

_____

_____

_____

_____

Events that appear to be quite miraculous begin to happen to me once I fully trust the answer to my desire has already been worked out, and then let go of how it will happen.

Through deep breathing or meditation and connecting with my heart energy, I am feeling more connected to my true nature and I've begun to see everything through the eyes of love. This is the secret to setting myself free from any struggle, and allows my dreams to manifest more easily. It feels easier to see the good in myself and in all situations. I now see any potential problem as an opportunity for growth. In doing so, my days are filled with the joy of...

_____

_____

_____

_____

_____

_____

_____

_____

_____

_____

_____

_____

_____

_____

_____

_____

_____

_____

_____

_____

I have a great love residing in my heart, and like a magnet, it attracts beautiful people, places and things into my life. I am feeling so fortunate and full of love for who I am. The bigger my unconditional love for anything I pay attention to, the higher my vibration, and the more I invite lovely circumstances into my life.

In my mind's eye, and with my intention, I've made my energy or energetic field as big as my desires. I am more radiant and magnetic than ever. What connections am I making? What are all the great things that are on their way to me? What am I magnetic to right now?

_____

_____

_____

_____

_____

_____

_____

_____

_____

_____

_____

_____

_____

_____

_____

_____

_____

_____

_____

_____

_____

_____

_____

 I am filling my shoes with the energy that attracts my deepest desires. Abundance is natural to me. It's my birthright. I'm always in the vicinity of it, and it's now getting easier to let it in. All day, every day.

To keep my wealth circulating, I consider it mine and allow it to flow freely in and out of my life. I offer whatever gifts, words, or thoughts I truly wish to offer from the heart. I graciously receive gifts and compliments. I love and appreciate what I have and make use of it. I bless the money that goes out and the person or service receiving it, with gratitude. Some examples of these experiences are...

_____

_____

_____

_____

_____

_____

_____

_____

_____

_____

_____

_____

_____

_____

_____

_____

_____

_____

_____

_____

_____

How much wealth I receive is directly related to how much I allow, believe, and expect it to happen for me. To feel more worthy and abundant, I practice the feeling of self-love and acceptance. What's not to love? I am so very fortunate to be who I am and I wouldn't want to be anyone else!

We gave you an invisible crown to wear to strengthen your connection with us. We're receiving your pure signal more clearly now. You should be hearing more of our messages for when to go somewhere, call someone, or do something in particular. We're offering some pretty brilliant ideas for you to follow up on that will bring you much joy. We know you're open to it. Just remember to quiet your mind a few minutes a day to give us more opportunity to beam in. If this made you smile, good. That brings us in even closer. What reasons are you finding to smile and laugh more these days?

_____

_____

_____

_____

_____

_____

_____

_____

_____

_____

_____

_____

_____

_____

_____

_____

_____

_____

_____

_____

_____

_____

_____

 I am easily led by my inner spirit and source energy. It is the path to my greatest joy. How much more fun and opulence am I able to attract into my life? There's no end to it.

Day 40 _____

I have a best friend who has the exact same desires I have, and I can easily and objectively see what they can do to attract them. What are all the things I would tell them to do, or not do, in order to align with their desired reality?

_____
_____
_____
_____
_____
_____
_____
_____
_____
_____
_____
_____
_____
_____
_____
_____
_____
_____
_____
_____
_____
_____

 I have made the invitation known, and I am now creating this reality for myself, if or when desired. How much more can I align with these positive changes in the days or weeks ahead? I am open to letting this happen for me in joyful and comfortable ways.

A WISH Moment for Inspiration
Words Inspire Spiritual Harmony

My desires want me as much as I want them. I *am* my desires. My desires are a part of me. We are finding our way to each other. My power to manifest what I want is enhanced by my belief and expectation and any thoughts, emotions or energy I hold around them.

What are the most powerful words I'm using to align with them? What if all I needed to do to add that extra magic for manifesting my wishes and dreams was to use the power of suggestion and ask myself really good questions? Questions that propose all that's possible for me? Such as how much better can I get at manifesting?

What if it works better than affirmations for me? What if I knew that my mind instantly wants to answer the question and starts to find ways to create the reality for me? If this works for others, why not me?

So what are all the ways I can ask for my desire in the form of a question that will prompt an answer from my mind, as well as the universe? I could ask questions like...

How does it feel to allow myself to feel limitless and create so much more abundance in my life now? When did I become so magnetic to my desires?

Why am I suddenly so decisive, determined, and diligent in my quest for more joy, love, and prosperity in my life? When did I start feeling so worthy and deserving of everything I could ever want? And how much more am I able to just sit back, relax, and enjoy the whole journey along the way?

How much better can I get at using visualization and my imagination to help my manifestations along? What if I just did that for fun but knew they would come to fruition either way?

What if I had the controls to my manifestations and could make things happen more quickly? What if I could start saying that I'm a success story and become one? What if I could manifest my ideal career now? How does it feel to be going to my new workplace starting tomorrow?

What if I believed I could finish this project in the amount of time I wanted to do it in, and it happened? What if I could accomplish *everything* I wanted to get done this week and had a lot of time left for fun?

What if my attention to anything is making it bigger? What if I felt money *crammed* in my hand or pocket every day and attracted more of it *to* me? Isn't it *always* there when I want it? It is when I see it that way.

What if I never felt the absence of *anything* and only focused on what I know is *now* on its way to me *at this moment*?

What if I could release anything that isn't aligned with my true desires, and replace it with amazing new memories or ideas, and did so easily and effortlessly? How many more like-minded people can I attract by thinking of how much I appreciate the great conversations we'll have together?

How did I become so brave and adventurous? Why do I feel so free to be myself now? When did I start feeling so satisfied with everything in my life?

How does it feel when I allow myself to feel fearless and free? How much more fearless and free can I feel in my mind and body? What if I could ask myself this so often that I felt an *incredible* shift in my energy, and began feeling more confident in doing *anything* I desire to do at any given moment? And said what I want to say the *moment* I wanted to say it? And felt empowered to be who I was born to be?

What if I use my natural talents to do what makes me happy in life, and it ends up bringing value to others? Not that it has to, but how good does that feel to have others gain an understanding about themselves just by seeing how authentically I live *my* life?

What if I decided that everything I touch will be a guaranteed success? And then believed it so much that I make it true? What if I was told that since I was a baby? How likely do you think it would come true then? I can decide to start telling myself that right now. Any thought I think daily or regularly until it becomes a belief that I feel with all my heart, must become my reality.

How does it feel to be so good at feeling like my dream is a part of me that it can't help but become so? How does it feel to be so magnetic to my desires that I'm getting what I want, or even something better? I believe I am magnetic to all my wishes and dreams because...

_____

How did I learn to be so good at being deliberate about my intentions? Why am I feeling so certain that everything in my life is becoming better every day in *every* way?

I love how wonderful, rich, and alive I feel. I love how invincible I feel. I am in the qualities of my happy, healthy, abundant life. I practiced it, and it became natural to me. I am in the qualities of someone who's often amused and having fun. I smile and laugh more. I celebrate who I am every day. I feel so very fortunate. And I'm always getting the equivalent of the vibration I'm offering. I have the qualities of those I wish to invite into my life. I am in the qualities of being in love. I am in the character of a lover of life with a generous heart. I am in the qualities of someone who's intuitive and decisive. I am in the qualities of my ease with all that is. I am in the qualities of my confidence and success, and most of all, joy. What am I choosing to be or have or do from this point forward? From now on, with the best of my intentions, I *choose* to feel, be, have, or do...

_____

_____

_____

_____
_____
_____
_____
_____
_____
_____
_____
_____
_____
_____
_____
_____
_____
_____
_____
_____
_____
_____
_____
_____
_____
_____

I decided, and it's done. I am focused and unstoppable in my spirit of abundance. I am practicing the feeling of anything I wish to achieve until I make it mine. I know who I am and what I want more clearly every day. I see every day as a fresh start with newly defined desires and acquired skills and qualities. I am creating the abundant life I was born to live. I'm taking the path to my greatest joy and wellbeing. And I deserve it!

The following is instilled in my mind and I feel it with *all* my heart:

By nature, I have the ability to be and have and do all that I desire. As I am true to my nature, I'm feeling the way I'm meant to feel. I am in love with life. I am confident and at ease. I am in the mindset of abundance, and I am limitless.

Fill this page with words of love and appreciation for anything and everything you are thankful for. Be sure to include everything you love about yourself.

Abundance

Freedom

Fun

Thank You

Happiness

Wellbeing

Love

 What if I could see everything in a way that benefits me and my wellbeing? I love feeling happy and free. All day, every day. This is what I choose for myself.

You're being challenged to a hundred days of singing a song, aloud or in your mind, that tells the story of how you want to live your life. It's a manifesting technique that others have used and brought their dreams to fruition. Create a song that states your desired reality in a few sentences, and then repeat them a couple more times. Come back to this page each day to practice singing it silently, until you've memorized it. The idea is to get it running in your mind until it's second nature and comes automatically. It's helpful to feel as though you're breathing in the energy of that reality as you're singing it in your mind. The beginning of a sentence might be: I am now achieving, I am now receiving, I am now aligning with, or I am now manifesting...

_____

_____

_____

_____

_____

_____

_____

_____

_____

_____

_____

_____

_____

_____

_____

_____

_____

_____

_____

_____

 With childlike abandon, I am impressing these desires on my subconscious mind, and it will naturally want to assist me in creating it. I am also replacing any unwanted thoughts or erasing unwanted images from my subconscious. I can even think of this song to redirect any negative thoughts, as needed.

You are your own boss at your company and are now able to delegate some tasks to your incredible new team. What are you passing on to them, and what's the most fun or interesting part you're keeping for yourself?

_____
_____
_____
_____
_____
_____
_____
_____
_____
_____
_____
_____
_____
_____
_____
_____
_____
_____
_____
_____
_____
_____
_____
_____

I am using my imagination to explore pretty unique circumstances, and it's leading to new ideas that align with my particular desires. All of this is creating more for me. More self-discovery. More creativity. More abundance. And wouldn't it be nice if it turned into way more fun than I ever imagined?

I'm walking into the bank right now to withdraw money. It's for the amount that covers any balances owed, plus any amount I want for myself this month, and a gift for someone in my family, just because I can. *Draw a picture of your withdrawal slip and fill it out. Close your eyes and imagine the teller counting it out in your hand. Now draw receipts for anything owed and stamp them "Paid in Full." Close your eyes again and see your family member's response to your gift as you put the stack of cash in their hand. See yourself spending what you took out, followed immediately by new income refilling your unlimited bank account.* It's falling from the sky and dropping right at my feet. My relief feels like...

_____

_____

_____

_____

_____

_____

_____

_____

_____

_____

_____

_____

_____

_____

_____

_____

_____

_____

_____

_____

 Watch out, a big wad of hundreds is coming your way and might hit you in the head. Oh, do forgive us. What we really want to say is, keep yourself and your head out of the way. There's nothing for you to think about. It's done. We'll take care of the details.

Someone just moved in next door and you've been introduced to a friend who helped them move in. It's the answer to one of your life's wishes. It may be for a job opportunity or a relationship or something else. Write the story of how it played out from the moment you saw them.

_____

_____

_____

_____

_____

_____

_____

_____

_____

_____

_____

_____

_____

_____

_____

_____

_____

_____

_____

_____

_____

_____

_____

 The universe may bring things to you in the simplest way, and often the most unexpected way. But its capabilities are of great magnitude and beyond limitation.

I've started feeling so lighthearted and have been humming and singing and laughing more of the time. I knew it was a good way to raise my vibration, so I made a point to create joy and laughter throughout my day. Before long, I noticed it happening more often without even trying. This was a sign that I was aligning with an abundance mindset and at some point my desires would come along. I felt certain they would and went about my merry way, and things started to manifest. I am thankful for all of my desires coming to me so easily because...

_____

_____

_____

_____

_____

_____

_____

_____

_____

_____

_____

_____

_____

_____

_____

_____

_____

_____

_____

_____

_____

_____

_____

 The law of attraction governs all things, so the quality of my life is equal to the quality of my consistent thoughts and emotions. And I'm getting it right!

Your wealth belt is getting heavy without use, and you need to unload some of it. Making use of it will move the energy, circulate the wealth, and bring more back to you. What are you spending this wealth energy on? It could be in the form of money, giving out gifts or genuine compliments, affection, or even doing some exercise or favorite activity. Have you been saving an activity for a rainy or sunny day? I am using my limitless energy and resources to...

_____
_____
_____
_____
_____
_____
_____
_____
_____
_____
_____
_____
_____
_____
_____
_____
_____
_____
_____
_____
_____
_____

 As I release old or stagnant energy, more layers of abundance are being added to my belt. The more that goes out, the more comes in. I'm building a positive momentum and accumulative effects are boundless and rampant. There's no end to the fun I'm going to have.

Day 47 _____

I've gotten so good at feeling appreciation for anything I pay attention to that I'm inviting more good things into my life. Instead of seeing what's wrong, I'm seeing what's right, or taking my attention away from it. What are the new and improved experiences I imagine having? What kind of people, conversations, and situations am I enjoying now? My favorite experiences and why I love them are...

_____
_____
_____
_____
_____
_____
_____
_____
_____
_____
_____
_____
_____
_____
_____
_____
_____
_____
_____
_____
_____
_____
_____
_____

 I love and appreciate my limitless supply of happiness! I'm happy where I am and excited for what's to come.

I decided to quit my 9-5 job and start an online business, knowing I could work from anywhere in the world. What am I teaching or selling, and where am I travelling to, if desired? How does it feel to be my own boss? Do I miss anything about working the 9-5 job? Which feels better? There's no wrong answer. What feels right to me is always my best answer. Write all the answers, and then add a list of pros and cons for each choice.

_____

_____

_____

_____

_____

_____

_____

_____

_____

_____

_____

_____

_____

_____

_____

_____

_____

_____

_____

_____

_____

_____

My wishes and dreams are uniquely my own, and I believe they're all happening for me at the perfect time, and in the best way for everyone involved. What's rightly mine is finding its way to me.

I play a game where every time I see a gold car, which is a color associated with good fortune, I imagine that I've just achieved one of my dreams. I decide which dream, and then imagine having a champagne toast with a friend to celebrate. I've been doing this for a couple months now and I started seeing gold cars everywhere I go. I am attracting, with ease, more of anything I frequently pay attention to. The dreams I think of must be coming along as well then. So what else do I want to make a game of or think about often and manifest?

_____

_____

_____

_____

_____

_____

_____

_____

_____

_____

_____

_____

_____

_____

_____

_____

_____

_____

_____

_____

_____

_____

 I love having a genuine appreciation for all the magical things that are now being arranged on my behalf. I expect good things to happen to me and those around me with effortless ease.

You're with your friend or significant other and you're planning your bi-annual vacation. Close your eyes and imagine where you're going, what you're doing, and the conversation you're having about it. And then write out the details.

_____

_____

_____

_____

_____

_____

_____

_____

_____

_____

_____

_____

_____

_____

_____

_____

_____

_____

_____

_____

_____

_____

If you're open to adding fuel to your imagination, and you don't mind doing something silly: stand up and sway from side to side and swing your hips, then add your arms...because that's how you'd be acting when you're getting excited for a trip. For further enhancement, close your eyes, continue swaying: sip on that cold drink, dip your toes in the ocean, feel the breeze and mist on your face, and lastly, have a conversation about it with the person you intend to go with, right out loud. The motion will create more emotion in your imagination. What if it works?

If you can muster it and you're comfortable with it, fill this page with words of appreciation for your favorite parts about previous jobs, relationships, projects, or other experiences that didn't turn out as you hoped. Putting your attention on the best qualities of anything you experience is a great way to open the doors for your brightest future in all areas of your life.

Abundance

Freedom

Fun

Thank You

Happiness

Wellbeing

Love

 You're becoming a magnet for all your favorite things put together!

Day 51 _____

If you're comfortable with it, write a letter to someone you would like to improve your relationship with, or imagine having a conversation with them (or a symbol of them). Tell them how you would like things to be between you, and your favorite things about them. Tell them what you would like them to appreciate about you, and how you'd like your next meeting to go, or anything else you wish.

_____
_____
_____
_____
_____
_____
_____
_____
_____
_____
_____
_____
_____
_____
_____
_____
_____
_____
_____
_____
_____
_____

As I make peace with what has been and change my energy around a relationship, I am creating change in the outcome. Repeat this process as often as it feels good, and again right before seeing them. Watch and notice the improvement that comes. I am opening doorways on my path to more joy.

I learned how to easily and effortlessly finish projects I've started. I decided to do one small step at a time, and before long I built up a powerful momentum. It became so satisfying to complete any part of it by the end of my day or week, that I couldn't stop until it was done. Now it feels completely natural to me. *Tell a friend or family member how this new practice has changed your life and increased your energy and abundance.*

_____

_____

_____

_____

_____

_____

_____

_____

_____

_____

_____

_____

_____

_____

_____

_____

_____

_____

_____

_____

_____

_____

 I am taking pressure off myself and letting things come more easily to me. This appears to be the key to letting the answers come, and it all leads to more joy. Life is as easy as I let it be.

Day 53 _____

You donated some money and didn't know at the time, but a big company provided an incentive prize to inspire more donations. Apparently you've been so fearless about money going out and more at ease about life that *you* ended up manifesting this grand prize. It's a dream home, and has every luxury imaginable. Another option is to pass on it for a million dollars. They're giving you one night in the house to decide. Who's the first person you'll tell? Draw the floorplan and put yourself in the picture. Describe your night's celebration in detail and how it feels to be there. Where is it and what's your favorite part? Which are you choosing and why? How does it change your life?

_____

_____

_____

_____

_____

_____

_____

_____

_____

_____

_____

_____

_____

_____

_____

_____

_____

_____

_____

_____

_____

 What's it like to be a winner? Or a master manifester? It's in your blood. Your time is coming. See it. Feel it. Taste it. Breathe it in.

Day 54 _____

I started a new habit of talking to my fears and facing them head on. I imagine that I have a conversation with them and in a short amount of time they seem to magically disappear. If it's something I'm afraid of doing, I see myself *doing* it with confidence and ease. I think acknowledging or accepting any fears I may have is resolving any issues associated with them. Things are now opening up in my life. Doors are opening. I am now fearless about... And to any fears I may have, or those I may not even be aware of, I say...

_____

_____

_____

_____

_____

_____

_____

_____

_____

_____

_____

_____

_____

_____

_____

_____

_____

_____

_____

_____

_____

_____

_____

 How does it feel to be so lighthearted and carefree that everything's going my way? All day every day.

You decided to catch up on paperwork and donate a bunch of unused things around the house and suddenly there's an influx of activity in the form of gifts, phone calls, emails, or checks in the mail. They all brought good news or lucrative opportunities, and your newfound crystal-clear clarity was a bonus. It's as though the decluttering process has opened up space for more good things to come, mentally and physically, as it does for so many. Imagine it now, and then list the details of each.

_____
_____
_____
_____
_____
_____
_____
_____
_____
_____
_____
_____
_____
_____
_____
_____
_____
_____
_____
_____
_____
_____
_____
_____
_____

As I set up an atmosphere of success, my abundant life begins to flow more freely. I receive many pleasant surprises, and some not so surprising, since I knew they were coming.

Day 56 _____

It's as though you're up above watching over your life on a roadmap. You can see how things line up on each person's path based on their vibrational frequency, and everyone's experience is quite different. Due to your consistently high frequency, your dazzling inner light is matching up with what you've been intending. You see where you are and you can see all your desires within miles of you. They're just around the corner. Close your eyes and watch as you and your desires find your way to each other, one at a time, until they are right in front of you. Describe the experience, as well as the quality and essence of the light you're in.

_____

_____

_____

_____

_____

_____

_____

_____

_____

_____

_____

_____

_____

_____

_____

_____

_____

_____

_____

_____

_____

 Now imagine walking up to each desire, touch them, and feel how it feels to be there with them and have them in your life. I am in the energy of my desires and they are in mine, and now we become one.

Ballroom dancing has become really popular again, and a friend of yours took lessons that really paid off. They're a phenomenal dancer now and can sweep anyone off their feet. What is one thing you fantasize about being able to do so well that you're the center of attention, even if only in your dreams? Close your eyes and visualize yourself doing it to perfection. Use your most playful imagination and tell the story of how it comes to life, how it feels, and the positive results and life experiences that come from doing it.

_____
_____
_____
_____
_____
_____
_____
_____
_____
_____
_____
_____
_____
_____
_____
_____
_____
_____
_____

I am newly inspired to step out of my comfort zone in whatever way I choose. I imagine myself accomplishing one of my goals, and it comes easily. My brain doesn't know the difference between what is real or imagined, so my vision and feeling of doing an action is a very powerful tool to create anything I wish.

Your inner spirit or natural intuition is constantly guiding you on a path to more joy and your emotions are a compass for the best direction to go in. Close your eyes, place your hands over your chest, right palm first, and tune into your heart center for a few minutes or so. Sense anything it's telling you and write down what first comes to mind. This may feel like your imagination, but if it feels good to hear it, it's a message made for you. What did you hear, and what are your favorite gifts you've been guided toward or given in life?

_____
_____
_____
_____
_____
_____
_____
_____
_____
_____
_____
_____
_____
_____
_____
_____
_____
_____
_____
_____
_____
_____

My joy and peace is in my heart and stays with me wherever I go. It's my home frequency. No matter where I go, who I'm with, or what I'm doing, I'm able to stay in a good-feeling place that's in harmony with my inner spirit.

I've been asked to attend an all-expense paid, week-long seminar at a remote location. Here are the details of where it is, what I'm choosing on the menu at which restaurants, what activities I take part in, what feels great about it, and what happens at the seminar that's never happened to me before...

_____

_____

_____

_____

_____

_____

_____

_____

_____

_____

_____

_____

_____

_____

_____

_____

_____

_____

_____

_____

_____

_____

_____

What if I knew I could always dine and shop without limitation? There's always enough and my supply is never depleted. If I believe it, I can create it. How much more abundant can I feel today and in the days ahead?

Day 60 _____

I am now attracting my true desires by thinking, speaking, and acting accordingly, as if I'm preparing to receive them at any moment. I am the master of my mind and my life, and I can have whatever I focus on. And I love that things are always working out for me. The things that I put my attention on and see working out for me are...

_____

_____

_____

_____

_____

_____

_____

_____

_____

_____

_____

_____

_____

_____

_____

_____

_____

_____

_____

_____

_____

_____

_____

_____

_____

I am allowing my life to flourish. I no longer doubt myself or feel unworthy of my desires. Every whim, every desire, every wish is fulfilled at the perfect time. The more I say something is working out for me, the more I believe it, the more attention I give it, and the more it becomes true.

A WISH Moment for Inspiration
Words Inspire Spiritual Harmony

I wished. I dreamed. I believe in all of it and expect it to come. I choose to trust and surrender and be more present in the many joys of life, and allow my abundance to flow. I know my vision is achievable, and I believe in it so much that it has no choice but to materialize.

Is there anything that I think I need to do or change about myself before I can achieve it?

I am deciding right now that no matter what I know, or don't think I know, I am capable of doing everything I desire. I have unique talents and gifts and the natural ability to accomplish anything I decide to do. What I seek is already within me and the answers will come.

How does it feel when all my words, thoughts, and actions are in keeping with the energy of the successful and joyful person I intend to be? The law of attraction is always responding to my vibration and consistent thoughts. I get myself into the best-feeling place I can be in every single day. I'm telling the story of who I choose to be on a continuous basis, and lack or limitation does *not* exist.

The more I say things like this to myself, the more my brain is being retrained with new thought patterns and washing away any old limiting beliefs that weren't mine to begin with. Here are the kinds of thoughts I like to practice now, and I do so each day with more and more determination:

I love being me. I love being in this body. I love living this life. I wouldn't want to be anyone else. I believe in myself. I feel the value of getting to be who I am. I love the way I think and feel. I love knowing what I know. I love that I cherish my thoughts and ideas. I love when I let myself revel in the spirit of fun. I love knowing that I can do anything.

I can choose how I want to feel. I can choose what I want to do. I get to choose what I believe and what I invite into my life. I can create any feeling and any reality I want to exist in. I am using my creative mind to be what I want to be. I can see it, feel it, taste it, and touch it, and it's mine.

I am now achieving blissful wellbeing. I am now feeling happy and free. I am now achieving all that I wish for. I love that I gave myself permission to have as much fun as I can have and to know that is all I need to do to get to the point of inspired action and achieve my dreams!

My consistent thoughts are creating my reality. So I focus on the spectacular things around me.
I am in the present joy that surrounds me.
And that's the key to attracting what I want.
Why is it so easy for me to do this now?
Why is it so easy for me to believe in my dreams now?

Fill this page with words of appreciation for your gifts and talents, your work, coworkers or employees, your accomplishments, or for those who've positively influenced you, and more.

Abundance

Freedom

Fun

Thank You

Happiness

Wellbeing

Love

 I am paving my way to a lovely future for myself. It just keeps getting better, and way more fun!

Just like in the movies, an angel appeared and told me I had three routes I could take in my life right now. They presented three choices or directions I could take, and each one creates a completely different outcome for my life. One path is what one might call safe or secure. Another is a bit daring and completely out of my comfort zone, and has its ups and downs, but ultimately provides me with major personal growth, which eventually leads to such elation. And the last one is beyond my wildest dreams, easy peasy, but results in my boredom and continually seeking a more purposeful life. Imagine taking each route and which one feels better to be living in one to three years. Write out the details, including how it changes your life, good or bad, and then choose one.

_____

_____

_____

_____

_____

_____

_____

_____

_____

_____

_____

_____

_____

_____

_____

_____

_____

_____

_____

_____

_____

_____

I have inherited the limitless abundance of the universe and now all things that are rightly mine are drawn to me like a magnetic force that cannot be severed.

Yay! One of your biggest dreams just came true. Someone just placed the finished product or a symbol of it in your hand. Perhaps it's a photograph of your desired end result, an award, or letter delivering the good news. Close your eyes and imagine it in your hands and how it feels to have it and use it or be in the energy of it. Breathe it in and see yourself sharing the news with someone you know. How does it feel to have achieved it, and how has it changed your life? What was the best part of getting there?

_____

_____

_____

_____

_____

_____

_____

_____

_____

_____

_____

_____

_____

_____

_____

_____

_____

_____

_____

_____

_____

_____

 Thank you for this dream coming to life...this or something better than this, at the perfect time and in a great way. Isn't the journey to getting there the best part? And knowing it continues...

When did I start feeling the magic of love and source in my heart and doing all of my actions under that influence or under that spell? In each area of my life, and all throughout my day or even my life, the things I am doing or intend to do differently in this wonderfully bold and magnetic state of mind are...

_____

_____

_____

_____

_____

_____

_____

_____

_____

_____

_____

_____

_____

_____

_____

_____

_____

_____

_____

_____

_____

_____

_____

What if I could double the ease in my mind and joy in my heart and become an unstoppable force in my life? Close your eyes and ask, "how much more harmony and magnetism can I feel in my body and my breath?" and give your body time to respond. As I master my emotions, I easily master the energy I give out and become a master manifester.

I recently woke up from a dream that gave me what felt like a brilliant idea. I just know it will be a success if I follow up on it, even if it doesn't seem to make any logical or practical sense. My infinitely wise self never bases a hunch on that. So I moved forward on it with fearless faith, and two months later the results came in for this creation I made. It's a life-changing product or service. What is it and how is it affecting those who are experiencing it for the first time? The list of reviews are saying...

_____

_____

_____

_____

_____

_____

_____

_____

_____

_____

_____

_____

_____

_____

_____

_____

_____

_____

_____

_____

_____

_____

_____

I trust in the power of my words, thoughts, intentions, and energy. I am using them to the best of my ability, and effortlessly creating the life I wish for.

Out of the blue my boss told me they really like my creative style and taste and asked if I would buy holiday gifts for their entire family and relatives on their behalf. They're giving me ten thousand dollars to spend, and I get two thousand of it. The only rule is that I take a full day off work and spoil myself with every penny before the day's end. What kind of gifts *thrill* me to buy that I know will truly make someone's day or even their year? And what splendor will I entertain myself with on my day off?

_____

_____

_____

_____

_____

_____

_____

_____

_____

_____

_____

_____

_____

_____

_____

_____

_____

_____

_____

_____

_____

_____

_____

 Imagine it now. Being at ease and doing what I please comes easily to me, and puts me in the energy of my limitless nature and abundant life.

Day 66 _____

It's your wishes and dreams talking. It's time for you to let us in. Allowing yourself to love and appreciate who you are, where you are, and where you're going is a great way to do it. Being more in the energy of the wonderful things to come is very powerful. Think of them being minutes away, hours away, easily attainable, and always within reach. You are drawn to us as strongly as your desire is impelling us to you. If you could breathe in the energy of each of your desires right now, what are the words or phrases to describe how it feels to have us be a part of you? Write to each of us about how it would feel. First close your eyes, and for each desire: see it and feel it, and breathe it in.

_____

_____

_____

_____

_____

_____

_____

_____

_____

_____

_____

_____

_____

_____

_____

_____

_____

_____

_____

_____

My desire for what I want and its desire for me is such a strong force that nothing can break it. And my unwavering faith is the powerful leverage from which my desires are revealed.

I am radiating the energy that matches the desires that I want to receive, and that I expect to receive with certainty. I am now receiving my heart's desires with no further effort on my part. Who am I in this energy? Who am I continually becoming? How would the universe or my inner being describe who I've become? *Step into our shoes. In every aspect of yourself, in mind, body, and spirit, and in every area of your life, we would say you are...*

_____

_____

_____

_____

_____

_____

_____

_____

_____

_____

_____

_____

_____

_____

_____

_____

_____

_____

_____

_____

_____

_____

_____

 You are one with your universe, and therefore one with your fortune. There are signs of abundance all around you and continually flowing to you. With intention, open your mind and heart to receive it, and like stardust it pours over you.

Congratulations! We're giving you an award for one year of success in doing something that's good for you. It's not something you feel you should do, but something you fully enjoy. This is creating the most happiness and highest energy for you. Your mind, body, and spirit come into harmony with one another when you do it as well. What is it, why do you do it, and what do you love about it?

_____

_____

_____

_____

_____

_____

_____

_____

_____

_____

_____

_____

_____

_____

_____

_____

_____

_____

_____

_____

_____

 In my world, there are no rules. I make the rules. I get to decide. I'm in charge. And I choose to do what I love. Why is it so easy for me to feel happy and love the life I'm creating?

Day 69 _____

I am now preparing for my desired or newly improved relationship to manifest. If they were arriving tomorrow, what am I doing to prepare myself, mentally and physically? I have made room in my life for this desire, and I'm giving out the energy that attracts it. My environment and I are in the qualities and energy of...

_____
_____
_____
_____
_____
_____
_____
_____
_____
_____
_____
_____
_____
_____
_____
_____
_____
_____
_____
_____
_____
_____
_____

I am day-dreaming this desire into my reality. I can see them, feel them, love and appreciate them, and look forward to them, as well as the newly improved current relationship, if applicable or desirable. I am holding a place for the person who's lined up with the happy place I'm in.

You went online and ordered your immediate needs and wants, and most gratifying wish list. See the truckload that's being dropped off. There are one hundred boxes. What in the world did you get? And what's the look on your face or your family's faces when it arrives? Write down what you got, and then close your eyes and imagine putting it all away, wherever you're going to keep it. Be sure to include stuff that's just for fun, entertainment, or celebrations, or even donations, if desired.

_____
_____
_____
_____
_____
_____
_____
_____
_____
_____
_____
_____
_____
_____
_____
_____
_____
_____
_____
_____
_____
_____
_____
_____

If I can see myself having something and enjoying it, it's as good as done. There's more to life than material things, but I can have it all. Joy, wellbeing, love, and more prosperity. Universe, thank you for showing me signs that my emotions are on track with my true desires.

I am so thankful for new life experiences and opportunities that bring more like-minded friends, adventures, and all kinds of success. I'm thankful for what I am now easily achieving, and looking forward to the joy of...

Abundance

Freedom

Fun

Thank You

Happiness

Wellbeing

Love

 Fully trust and believe that all is well and your desires are on their way to you. There's no hard work to be done. Decide to simply enjoy life and let things be easy and fun for you.

Day 71 _____

I am now attuned to the harmony of my true nature and the limitless abundance of the universe. I desire it, and therefore I am. As I move forward in my fearless faith and purposely create my ideal reality, I am exhilarated with the expectation of my impending desires. As I see this vision from the universe's viewpoint and my abundant nature, I am looking forward to...

_____

_____

_____

_____

_____

_____

_____

_____

_____

_____

_____

_____

_____

_____

_____

_____

_____

_____

_____

_____

_____

_____

_____

 When I view my life as a co-creation with the universe, I see through the eyes of my limitless and true nature, and know how powerful I am.

My wealth belt has become so long with extra layers being added to it, that it's beginning to look like a skirt or a kilt. Now I imagine it slapping against my legs as I walk, with strips of hundreds flapping about that represent my ongoing freedom and abundance, and it makes me laugh out loud. Bizarre as it may be, I welcome the image coming to mind because anything that amuses me instantly raises my vibration and attracts more of what I want. What are other ways to amuse myself, especially when something worries me? Can I see a zero balance due and a flash image of cash stuffed into the envelope when I receive a bill? I bet I can think of something more interesting. For each issue that I consider unwanted, I now see it in a comical way, such as...

_____
_____
_____
_____
_____
_____
_____
_____
_____
_____
_____
_____
_____
_____
_____
_____
_____
_____
_____
_____
_____

 As I amuse myself about anything that used to worry or annoy me, I am releasing resistance and inviting more riches into my life.

Day 73 _____

One day you were taking a shower and an amazing idea came to mind so you mentioned it to an acquaintance that invested in other business ventures. They loved the idea and wanted to partner with you and run the business. You can be a silent partner or in charge of any department you wish. What's the product or service and what position in the company would you choose and why? How does this new venture change your life?

_____
_____
_____
_____
_____
_____
_____
_____
_____
_____
_____
_____
_____
_____
_____
_____
_____
_____
_____
_____
_____
_____
_____
_____

 I am more open to seemingly miraculous surprises every day. Anything is possible, and endless choices are available to me.

You and a group of others have been asked to do a talk in the school auditorium of a local grammar school. The school received a grant to organize the event and publish a textbook of the content to distribute to all schools nationwide. It's meant to be a handbook of valuable insights that will provide a roadmap to a life full of joy and success. What would you like to instill in all the children that you wish you had known before adolescence or adulthood? Or believed about yourself, even?

_____
_____
_____
_____
_____
_____
_____
_____
_____
_____
_____
_____
_____
_____
_____
_____
_____
_____
_____
_____
_____
_____

My self-esteem and resiliency increases every day. I practice observing myself and others for the limitless potential that exists within all of us.

The universe has been working diligently to bring about your biggest wish. We have utilized people, conversations or situations as messengers on your path. They're put there to provide you with hints or details on the right direction to take at every turn, yet they may seem random. Perhaps you've overheard something or experienced it directly, but the message is clear and always arrives in time. The universe is never late, and no opportunity is ever missed. What signs have you noticed, and what do you think this guidance is trying to tell you? And what is the obvious next step toward your biggest wish?

_____

_____

_____

_____

_____

_____

_____

_____

_____

_____

_____

_____

_____

_____

_____

_____

_____

_____

_____

_____

_____

_____

The less disturbed you are by what could appear to be a standstill or an unfortunate situation, the more those problems seem to miraculously fade away. They may even be disguised as a way to show you a new direction to take. Decide to stay calm and trust that we're aware of your needs and wants and it's all being worked out for you.

I became an expert in my field and now I work as a highly paid consultant for just a few hours a week. This is beyond my wildest dreams. I have a feeling my playful side brought it about. Several months ago, I wanted to inspire myself to attract clients so I hung some hundred dollar bills at the top of my kitchen window, all fanned out like sunshine. Every time I walked by it, it made me smile to myself, and I became really comfortable with the idea of having more money. What other ways could I inspire myself or be silly enough to put myself in the range of emotions that attract my desires?

_____

_____

_____

_____

_____

_____

_____

_____

_____

_____

_____

_____

_____

_____

_____

_____

_____

_____

_____

_____

_____

I am playful and purposeful and positive outcomes and opportunities find me. I'm using my creative imagination and energy like a magnetic force that attracts what I'm thinking of. Or something better.

Day 77 _____

You entered a contest and won. It was like no other contest you've heard of and the final outcome is beyond your expectations. There are surprises they didn't divulge in the event guidelines. An enormous gym bag has been stuffed full of your winnings and is, at this moment, being delivered to your front door and dumped out in front of you. It is filled with things you've wanted, and additional luxuries you're not typically into, but are surprisingly enticing. What is all of it? Write a list and then see yourself enjoying it or sharing it.

_____

_____

_____

_____

_____

_____

_____

_____

_____

_____

_____

_____

_____

_____

_____

_____

_____

_____

_____

_____

_____

_____

_____

 How does it feel to try new things and lavish yourself in the energy of what's to come? Here's your new mantra: I'm a winner! Repeat daily. It's coming true.

Day 78 _____

I decided to demonstrate my openness to hear what my intuition has to say by having imaginary conversations with a symbol that represents the wisest part of me (the one that has all the answers to anything I could ever want to know). And the results were extraordinary. Insights, answers, and brilliant ideas started flowing more frequently. I also started to feel deeply connected to my core self and it feels so good. It's a feeling of being whole and secure, with a tremendous sense of wellbeing and fearlessness. In a conversation with my symbol today, I ask and intend... Also, with this empowering energy, I feel able to...

_____
_____
_____
_____
_____
_____
_____
_____
_____
_____
_____
_____
_____
_____
_____
_____
_____
_____
_____
_____
_____
_____

My inner spirit guides me to align with my true self. I am guided and protected as I follow my heart and intuition or anything that feels good to me. This inner source knows what I want and how to align with it, and is never apart from me.

Day 79 _____

For every dream big or small you have, write one or more sentences for each one as though it's already taken place. Begin each sentence with I love feeling, I love being, I love having, and so on.

_____
_____
_____
_____
_____
_____
_____
_____
_____
_____
_____
_____
_____
_____
_____
_____
_____
_____
_____
_____
_____
_____
_____

 I practice saying and feeling this or something like it, and I easily attract my wishes and dreams. I give my undivided attention to the desires I have that feel the best, and positive outcomes always follow my positive thoughts and emotions.

There's one big or small step you can take to show your faith in a desire working out for you. What is it? This could be as little as writing a checklist on what to pack, buying travel size bottles, or choosing restaurants to visit for the trip you're wishing to go on. Or how about researching and test-driving that vehicle? Doing anything that prepares you for your desired outcome is an act of faith that has the power to set things in fast forward mode. For each of my desires, I could...

_____
_____
_____
_____
_____
_____
_____
_____
_____
_____
_____
_____
_____
_____
_____
_____
_____
_____
_____
_____
_____
_____

The next thing you know someone's asking you to take a trip that they won, or better. Ta-da! Things like this have happened for people. That's how the universe works...in very mysterious ways. And sometimes when you least expect it.

A WISH Moment for Inspiration
Words Inspire Spiritual Harmony

My reality is becoming what I wish it to be, what I think it to be, what I imagine it to be, and what I feel it to be. In essence, it will always be what I expect or believe it to be. I love that I get to be directly involved in creating my life. I have creative control. I have the authority to decide how I want my life to unfold.

And I've been feeling energy moving. I feel clarity flowing. I feel that I'm in my element. All forces are moving in order to bring me every desire, and I'm ready. I am in the energy of all the qualities that are necessary for my alignment with my desires.

I see my future as unlimited potential and I know that I'm achieving my desires. I'm not concerned with how I'll get there. I just know I will. I always do. And anything I want to make possible for me, I just start saying that it's possible. And my faith in myself and my strong desire will always persevere. I'm not fazed by any bumps along the way. I never fear failure because the concept of failure doesn't exist in my world.

All my life experiences are a success when I know they're moving me forward and leading me to the next step on my path. When something doesn't work out, I assume there's something even better to come, and feel thankful that I'm now available for that to happen.

And when it comes to home life or the work I'm doing now, no matter how little I've done or how much time I've spent on the smallest of details, if it's done well in *my* estimation, I've had a successful day. I am certain the actions I'm taking are going to result in only the most positive outcomes for me.

How does it feel to look at it this way, and to know that I'm becoming more successful as I think of it?

What's it like when I'm aligned with my inevitable success:

> I am in sync with my vision.
> I believe I have the know-how to achieve my goals.
> I keep my vision in mind as I take inspired action.
> I have complete faith that I will reach my full potential, whether that's becoming successful in business or enjoying more time with my family.
> I make the most of anything I'm doing *now*, and ensure only the best outcomes for my future.
> I put my heart into my work.
> I put my heart into my relationships.
> I truly appreciate the parts I like about everything I do.
> I stay open to new and improved circumstances.
> And know that I deserve them.

Why is it suddenly so easy for me to live fearlessly, courageously, happily, wholeheartedly, and powerfully?

How does it feel to think and feel and act like the person I was born to be?

> It means I'm being genuine. I'm being passionate.
> I'm living my life with purpose. It means I'm being me.
> The raw and unadulterated me. The invincible, successful, freedom-seeking, doesn't-know-the-word-failure me.

All that I seek is seeking me, and what's meant to be will be.

What I want is working its way toward me. It's inevitably becoming mine. I am holding a mental conception of myself in the highest level of joy, wellbeing, and abundant prosperity. I am practicing it until it's all I know. *All* that I know to be true for me.

♡♡♡ HARMONY ~ LIMITLESS ~ ABUNDANCE ~ FEARLESS ~ FREEDOM ♡♡♡

Every one of these is now like the air I breathe. This is my powerful intention.

Today and every day, my powerful intentions are to be, have, or feel...

_____

_____

_____

_____

_____

_____

_____

_____

_____

_____

_____

_____

_____

_____

_____

_____

_____

Fill this page with words of appreciation for the limitless freedom and choices you're looking forward to as you align more every day with the naturally abundant person you truly are.

Abundance

Freedom

Fun

Thank You

Happiness

Wellbeing

Love

 I am open and receptive to all the gifts that life has to offer me. Life just keeps getting better. Every day, in every way. All good things are flowing my way, and I'm letting it in!

It's a year from now and all your wishes and dreams have come true. Describe a typical day and week in the life of your new reality, including how it feels.

_____

_____

_____

_____

_____

_____

_____

_____

_____

_____

_____

_____

_____

_____

_____

_____

_____

_____

_____

_____

_____

_____

When you wholeheartedly believe in us, and believe we will come, there's no need to repeat affirmations or visualize us. Do it for the fun of it, but know that all of this is inevitably happening for you one way or another. Your heart full of joy and harmony is letting it in, even if only in fleeting moments.

I have family scattered around the country, and every December we get together and each of us gets twelve gifts from whoever picked our name, one for every month of the year we will miss each other. Some are customized and some are related to our favorite color, sport, hobby, or birthday and zodiac-related. We open one and save the rest for each of the next eleven months. The idea is that we're with each other in spirit and the gift reminds us of that. The twelve gifts that would delight me and have the most meaning to me are...

_____

_____

_____

_____

_____

_____

_____

_____

_____

_____

_____

_____

_____

_____

_____

_____

_____

_____

_____

_____

_____

 I can have what I want in life, and won't settle for anything less. I am a special gift to the world, and just the right gifts that are personally made for me are being handed to me.

You decided to go out for dinner by yourself and ended up meeting someone at the next table. This is either someone you want to date or your significant other who wanted to surprise you. Either way, describe your dream date with them. Include what you're talking about, how they look and act, how you feel, and what you love about this perfect date night. And why are they just right for you?

_____
_____
_____
_____
_____
_____
_____
_____
_____
_____
_____
_____
_____
_____
_____
_____
_____
_____
_____
_____
_____
_____

A wonderful relationship is mine to have, and I am creating it. I envision this happening for us, and so it shall be.

What if I could be the person I was born to be and do what I love to do in my life? Right *now*? If it was like the air I breathe and I was already living my life as though it was true, if not already, how would I be acting and what would I be doing? What are some steps I could take now that will be demonstrating my faith that it is indeed who I am already. I *know* I am everything I need to be in order to do what I want to do. If there's something I've been wanting to create in my life, what is one thing I'm inspired to do every week that is a small step in that direction? The research, inquiries, purchases, or imaginings that put me in the energy of my inevitable future, are...

_____

_____

_____

_____

_____

_____

_____

_____

_____

_____

_____

_____

_____

_____

_____

_____

_____

_____

_____

_____

_____

_____

 I am now in the frame of mind of being and having and doing what I intend to do in my magnificent life.

Three years from now, you're a success story according to a local news channel and they want you to share your story to inspire others. They intend to broadcast it on a global network show which could mean all kinds of opportunities for you, even overnight. Close your eyes and see a flash of scenes over the next three years and then capture an image of the end result. Feel how you would feel when you're there. Now write out the script you'll be reading from as you do a video about your success story.

_____

_____

_____

_____

_____

_____

_____

_____

_____

_____

_____

_____

_____

_____

_____

_____

_____

_____

_____

_____

_____

_____

 I am being one with my dream. I am living it, breathing it, loving it, and making it mine. Yes, please, and thank you!

Day 86 _____

I feel that my energy is now higher and stronger than any negative forces or energy that's around me. I also have my emotions as a compass that tell me if one direction is better for me to go than another, I use it when I'm deciding what events or conversations I want to take part in. I notice I've been choosing the direction of...

_____
_____
_____
_____
_____
_____
_____
_____
_____
_____
_____
_____
_____
_____
_____
_____
_____
_____
_____
_____
_____
_____
_____
_____
_____

 I love that I get to decide what I want to experience in this abundant life. And the more I radiate positive energy, the more I attract positive people, conversations, and moments throughout my day. I'm creating more positive moments just by appreciating this one.

Day 87 _____

The path to your desired life experience, as you imagined or better, is straight ahead of you. Where does it lead to? Take us on a magnificent journey of your future. In five, ten or twenty years, what have you created in your life? There are three keys in your hand. Begin with telling us what they're for, and go from there.

_____
_____
_____
_____
_____
_____
_____
_____
_____
_____
_____
_____
_____
_____
_____
_____
_____
_____
_____
_____
_____
_____
_____

 How does it feel to be so good at feeling like my dream life is a part of me, that it can't help but become so?

Day 88 _____

For anything you ever wished or prayed for, there's no need to ask again when you have complete faith in it. Things are set in motion for you the moment you desire it. So rather than continue asking, which may keep it from coming, you can feel genuinely thankful it's on its way. Write a list of anything you'd like to hand over to the universe to orchestrate, and set this intention.

_____

_____

_____

_____

_____

_____

_____

_____

_____

_____

_____

_____

_____

_____

_____

_____

_____

_____

_____

_____

_____

_____

_____

When you stop searching and feel thankful for it being given to you, it will find you. Let yourself look forward to it and be in the energy of what's to come. What you asked for, or better.

I volunteered to work a booth for a broadway-like theater for a season and ended up with hundreds of tips. It's more cash than I've ever had on me at once, and I'm taking it to the bank. Since I ran out of room in my pockets, I crammed some into my boots. The thought of it amused me. It was even more hilarious when I got to the bank and had to keep pulling money out of my boots and my deep pockets. I had to keep going back to my boots for more until I finally had a pile on the counter. You should have seen the look on the teller's face. I gave her some of it for being so patient. Imagine this now. How does it feel to have a ridiculous amount of money on you, and who else are you spending it on, and why?

_____

_____

_____

_____

_____

_____

_____

_____

_____

_____

_____

_____

_____

_____

_____

_____

_____

_____

_____

_____

_____

My desire for abundance is aligned with what the universe wants for me. Universe, thank you for my limitless supply. I am open to giving and receiving gifts of all kinds. What is rightly mine is finding its way to me.

Day 90 _____

The more I allow my heart to lead me, the more I notice my energy and circumstances changing in the most glorious way. And I love when the universe and law of attraction shows me results of my positive thoughts and high-vibin' energy by way of signs or synchronicities. My favorite part about it and the signs I've been seeing, feeling, or experiencing are...

_____

_____

_____

_____

_____

_____

_____

_____

_____

_____

_____

_____

_____

_____

_____

_____

_____

_____

_____

_____

_____

_____

_____

_____

_____

 I am now attracting more experiences like this, or better! Just showing my belief and expectation or faith and trust that it's already on its way to me brings results, sometimes when I least expect them.

If it feels good to imagine us in your life without feeling that something is missing, we're closer than you think. Go merrily about your day as though we're already there. We're a part of who you are, and there's no turning back now. We're yours. All in perfect timing. *Tell us* (your goals and dreams, big or little and everything in between) what you love about each of us and how it makes you feel to have us in your life.

Abundance

Freedom

Fun

Thank You

Happiness

Wellbeing

Love

Yours Truly,

Your Wishes & Dreams

I finally see all the gifts and talents I have to offer. I'm feeling naturally confident and pretty certain of my ability to attract what I want into my life. I'm walking into a beautiful building and feeling pretty magnetic to any experience I'd like to have there. Is there a party, sporting event, or special occasion there? What would be the event of a lifetime to me, and what's happening there? Also, what are the talents I feel good about, and the words to describe my confidence?

_____

_____

_____

_____

_____

_____

_____

_____

_____

_____

_____

_____

_____

_____

_____

_____

_____

_____

_____

_____

_____

_____

_____

_____

 Universe, thank you for guiding me to thoughts that align me with my desires, and take me to places where I connect with like-minded people.

You've been asked by a business coach to join their support team. You would be the mindset coach their clients talk to when they're needing encouragement or accountability, or perhaps technical help. What's the business topic, and is this something you'd jump at or turn down? Would you leave your current job for this? Write the details of your first client call. If you turned it down, what offer would thrill you to get and why?

_____
_____
_____
_____
_____
_____
_____
_____
_____
_____
_____
_____
_____
_____
_____
_____
_____
_____
_____
_____
_____
_____

I am inspired to be the person I was born to be, doing what I love! And I love how much faith I have in the inevitable success of anything I choose to do that aligns with my heart's passion.

Day 93 _____

What if I believed that I am creating my life with the power of the universe, and knew that the universe powered my desires? And did everything to make it happen? If I wholeheartedly trusted this was so, how much more empowered or confident do I feel in taking that next step and achieving my goals and dreams? Let's decide what we're creating together. The all powerful universe and I are creating...

_____

_____

_____

_____

_____

_____

_____

_____

_____

_____

_____

_____

_____

_____

_____

_____

_____

_____

_____

_____

_____

_____

 I am practically dancing through life as I follow my heart's desire. I move forward in my fearless faith in my ability to create anything I desire.

Day 94 _____

You discovered another pocket in your wealth belt that holds a lasso. It's electromagnetic and it's there to remind you that you're always giving out a signal that attracts your reality. See it as a cord of light, and let it be an extension of you. With your intention and high-vibin' energy, it can reach out and connect to your desires and bring them into your life with its pure signal. What's it like to know your true power and energetically connect yourself to any desire and manifest it at will? I love letting my desires come to me easily because...

_____
_____
_____
_____
_____
_____
_____
_____
_____
_____
_____
_____
_____
_____
_____
_____
_____
_____
_____
_____
_____
_____
_____
_____

 I am one with my source energy, and therefore I am one with my wishes and dreams. I see all that I am attracting in the palm of my hand. What if it was here now? Get ready...

Day 95 _____

You started a project that challenges you to make wishes for people that you're going to see each day. And now you're noticing that you're enjoying your relationships and your day more, and perhaps you're even noticing that your wishes seem to be coming back to you in some way. If anything, what has improved in your typical day at work, home, or in your personal life? And what kinds of wishes are coming true for you?

_____

_____

_____

_____

_____

_____

_____

_____

_____

_____

_____

_____

_____

_____

_____

_____

_____

_____

_____

_____

_____

 I am radiant in my natural state of joy and appreciation, and all of life's gifts are drawn to me.

I love the feeling of freedom. Like when I'm about to leave for a spontaneous road trip and I see the road ahead of me but I don't yet know my destination. The possibilities of who or what I might encounter along the journey exhilarates me. What are my favorite kinds of people, conversations, places, and adventures to create fun with? And what would the freedom of an open road feel like?

_____
_____
_____
_____
_____
_____
_____
_____
_____
_____
_____
_____
_____
_____
_____
_____
_____
_____
_____
_____
_____

With thoughts like these, I'm practicing the feeling of freedom and fun, and creating more adventure and time for myself. I am looking forward to the whole journey that leads to all my desires. It's the best part.

What if my belief that I'm connected with the infinite intelligence of the universe brought about answers that led me to my highest path of more joy and prosperity, and were readily available to me in *this* moment, and *every* moment? How does it feel to be aware of these insights streaming in and continually flowing to me throughout my day? If I knew everything on the path ahead would be fabulously comfortable, exciting, and fun to do, what are some new directions I might take in my life?

_____

_____

_____

_____

_____

_____

_____

_____

_____

_____

_____

_____

_____

_____

_____

_____

_____

_____

_____

_____

_____

_____

Why is it now getting so easy to relinquish control of how things will come about, and allow the universe to do the work? I am letting myself feel happy and free and living the dream. I never feel the absence of what I want, for I know it's already mine.

When I'm in a wonderful mood and feeling very fortunate, it's the best time to think about my wishes and dreams. With some real enthusiasm, I want to say that:

The many things that make me feel fortunate to be who I am are...

_____

_____

_____

I love how good it feels to be...

_____

_____

_____

I love how good it feels to have...

_____

_____

_____

I feel so fortunate when I think of my future because...

_____

_____

_____

What's my favorite part about what I expect to happen for me in the months to come and why does it feel good to me? How will it change my life?

_____

_____

_____

_____

I am in the energy of the beauty and abundance that's all around me, and feeling fortunate and eager for more. I love being in the energy of a person who is having the time of their lives.

What are some powerful words I can use to describe myself when I'm feeling focused and unstoppable in my mindset of abundance? All I know is that the forward direction of my thoughts and desires are creating my best life, and it feels...

_____

_____

_____

_____

_____

_____

_____

_____

_____

_____

_____

When I am feeling focused and unstoppable in my spirit of limitless abundance:

All that I desire is flowing to me as I transform my thoughts.
All that I desire is flowing to me as I believe in me.
All that I desire is flowing to me as I believe in my limitless supply.
All that I desire is flowing to me as I make it a part of me.

This limitless feeling of abundance is a part of who I am.
I feel it flowing to me, and I expect it to keep flowing to me.
I only associate myself with words of joy and appreciation and my natural state of abundance now.
I am focused on a feeling of fearless trust in all things working out for me in seemingly miraculous ways, and always in the best possible way.

When I decide to achieve any goal and practice the feeling of what I want as though it's mine right now, it becomes so. I am now achieving a deeply satisfying life that supports my true desires and limitless nature.

 I love designing the life of my dreams! I am focused and unstoppable in my spirit of abundance. Why is it so easy for me to attract my desires now?

Day 100 _____

Write a letter from your future self, about one year from now, telling a detailed story of who you've become. Explain how good you're feeling about yourself, your life, or anything you wish, and why you appreciate it so much. This is a fun way to energetically connect with your desired outcome. Think of it like an invitation to bring this into your life, and you're just getting ready for it. As your energy aligns with it, it will begin to unfold and reveal itself. Bit by bit, piece by piece, or perhaps all at once. As you hoped, or even better!

Dear Self,

_____

_____

_____

_____

_____

_____

_____

_____

_____

_____

_____

_____

_____

_____

_____

_____

_____

_____

_____

_____

_____

 This is your new story. Coming soon! Just think of the possibilities that are waiting for you. You're a magnificent creator and all that you desire is inevitably becoming yours. Or something better!

One Last WISH Moment for Inspiration

Please enjoy Day 86 from my first book, *100 Days of Actions & Intentions to Create the Life You Wish For*. It seemed like an appropriate choice for this manifesting journal.

My Wishes Come True

The process of creating my life is *amazing* to me. I decide what I want. I hold a vision of it. I allow it to come. And I do this by having faith and trust that it *will*, as I stay in the feeling place of joy and appreciation.

And I love how it feels when I put myself in the life I'm creating. I'm really good at aligning my energies to anything I want. I just practice how it feels when it's a part of my life.

How does it feel to have all my wishes come true?

What if today was the first day of my life and all I knew was that I would be happy, healthy, and successful? It's the only thing I ever heard, and it's the only thing I ever tell myself. I believe it wholeheartedly, and there's nothing opposing it.

How do I think my life would go? Would it feel like I'm being the person I was born to be? I can do my best to feel how it feels to be me, as I step into that reality now, where all my wishes have come true.

Only they're not just wishes. I've sorted through my life experiences and discovered what I truly want out of life. I've spent much of my time contemplating the manifested version of my desires, and I hold a vision of it in my mind. I'm in the feeling place of it, and it's become a part of who I am. And I'm ready to bring it to life.

So let's say it's about a year from now, and I've manifested all that I desire. How does it feel to be living it? If I could be in the feeling place of a day in this life, what would it feel like?

_____

_____

How does it feel to have what I would call my perfect kind of day after all my desires have manifested?

Words can't do it justice, but I can say that I feel like I'm in such a blissful state of wellbeing and abundance. The only thing I know how to experience is joy. Everything in my life is easy. I have so much appreciation for the ability to live this life and be who I am.

I found a way to see everything in my life as easy, joyful, and prosperous. Things started to happen and before I knew it, I was living my dream. It happened more quickly than I expected. I expected a lot of good things, but thought it would take more time.

I attracted the house I wanted, the healthy relationships I wanted, the career success I hoped for, and all the big and little things in between. *And it keeps getting better!*

I feel able to do *whatever* I wish, *whenever* I want, with *whomever* I choose.

I feel a *tremendous* sense of freedom. I'm *quite* literally high on life.

My day starts and ends in the most *glorious* way, and my day is *filled* with activities that please me. Life keeps getting more interesting and exciting, and the opportunities for growth and more fun are *ongoing*.

Step into my life the way *I* see it. I'm in the *same* energy of my desires and I'm feeling the way I do when I *have* all of it. What does it *look* like? What does it *feel* like? I'm going to say it all right now.

A year from now...

My lifestyle is:

The best part about it is:

I feel _____ all the time.

My ideal partner is:

The best part about them is:

I feel _____ when I'm with them.

They feel _____ when they're with me.

My family is really happy about:

I would describe my house as:

I've made changes to:

I hired help to:

My career is:

I can see myself at work and I am:

I accomplished all of these goals:

I even learned to:

I have way more freedom to:

I have the time and money to:

The car I'm driving is a:

I love driving it because:

My new hobbies are:

My favorite thing to spend money on is:

I'm most excited about my new:

My favorite thing to touch in my house is:

The best aroma coming from the new kitchen is:

The best-tasting dish I frequently have at my favorite restaurant is:

I wanted all of this because:

I love thinking about all that I am now achieving, and it makes me feel:

One of the ways I believe I created this life is by seeing it in front of me, as though my life was a blank canvas and I had artistic control as its creator.

I would picture it and be thinking: I am walking toward me right now. I notice the look on my face and how I feel. I have an air of confidence about me. I'm always smiling as though I hold the secret to true happiness. And I really feel that I do. It appears to me and those I meet that I am happy and free. And I'm just being myself.

And in this vision I would see myself surrounded by all that I desired. And now I have it.

In my vision, I always look like I'm on top of the world. Why do I look this way?

> *Because I'm loving myself and loving the life I'm living.*
> *I diligently sought my ideal life by doing whatever I could do to stay in a frequent state of appreciation, joy, and abundance.*
> *I let myself be at ease often enough to allow wellbeing and abundance to flow. This, along with finding the feeling place where my desires became a part of me, invited this reality to me. And I couldn't be more thrilled.*

And I am now in the qualities and energy of a happy, healthy, and successful person.

So many people have used this to create their ideal life, and I'm doing it just as well or better. I'm going to keep doing it for every new desire I have. But only when it feels fun. My desires are happening either way.

How does it feel when I wake up one day and it has happened? I got my wish!

How does it feel to be where I want to be?
To feel the way I want to feel?
To be with who I want to be with?
To be doing what I set out to do?
To be successful in anything I do?
How does it feel to have created the life I dreamed of?
How do I feel when it's a part of me?

If I close my eyes right now I can take myself there and be in the feeling place of it. What does it look and feel like? Reach out and touch something in each of the places I go. Smell the aromas, taste the dinner, feel the breeze on my face, or the ocean water touching my toes, and more. What else would be happening? Think of it now.

I feel deeply satisfied right now. I'm in pure joy in nearly every moment of this life I'm designing. And it never ends. I keep adding to its magnificence. When I'm in this magical place, everything I wish for comes true. Only, it's not really magical, it's just me being me.

It's natural for me to get what I want. And it feels so natural to me when it arrives because I am in the energy of it now. I knew it would come. I patiently waited for it in delightful anticipation, and I enjoyed every moment that led up to it and knowing there's always more to come!

If desired, take a moment to reflect on the time you spent doing your morning intentions and working your way through this journal. Have you had any breakthroughs or noticed any energy shifts or improvements in your life, or even your relationships? Are you feeling any differently about yourself or your life?

_____

_____

_____

_____

_____

_____

_____

_____

_____

_____

Congratulations! You made it all the way to Day 100! Thank you for taking the time to do this for yourself.

This is what we wish for you:

You *know* that you are what you say and think and *believe* you are, and that *everything* you want to be is *already* within you. There may be a few layers to unveil, but it's *all* there. It's a part of you now. It's who you are. You will continue to discover more of your true self. And this lovely truth, *your* truth, is setting you free.

You're owning your power to think how you wish to think and feel how you wish to feel. All day, *every* day. You're keeping your attention on what you truly want for yourself and letting anything that *doesn't* align with your desires fade away.

You expect every day to bring you good news. You have a feeling that something wonderful is happening for you, and hold that thought forevermore.

You know that when you ask, we answer. We always hear you and respond to you, and you're easily receiving manifestations from your place of faith, trust, and expectation.

You're feeling happy where you are and excited for what's to come. You're playful and purposeful and letting positive outcomes and opportunities find *you*.

You're letting it be okay no matter where you're at and not fazed by anything that doesn't *appear* to be going your way. You hold a vision of your desired end result and have faith that everything is working out for you. In doing so, you're creating even better future outcomes.

You know that anytime you think a self-doubting or limiting thought that it's not how *we* see you, and that's why it feels uncomfortable for you. You easily dismiss those thoughts because you know they're not your true thoughts. They're not coming from your true self.

All you know is that you are complete and total wellbeing and limitless abundance. It's simply a thought you hold and make it your truth.

You're using the word "my" a lot. Instead of thinking of your desires as something you're trying to attain, you're owning what's yours. Your inner knowing is thinking "I *am* my desires. I *am* my wellbeing. I *am* my abundance. I *am* my limitless supply of health, wealth, and happiness. I *love* my life. I *love* my happy, healthy family. I *love* my new or improved relationship. I *love* my money."

You feel guided, guarded, and safe, and love is your home frequency. You're feeling confident, radiant, and naturally abundant as you go about your day.

For anything you wish to create, you imagine it, feel it, live it and breathe it, and know it's rightly yours to have, and expect it to come with effortless ease. There's no end to what you can attract to you and you know it fully with your whole heart. You're a magnet to all your life's wishes, and you know it and own it!

You continue to expand and grow in your conscious awareness. You're shining your light and sharing your many talents and gifts with the world.

Lastly, you value yourself and treat yourself as wonderfully as you would a dear friend.

And now we invite you to take the next hundred days and beyond to allow your own imagination and daydreaming to do its work naturally.

Frequently quieting your mind, as well as using your imagination with purpose is activating higher consciousness and initializing a continuous stream of insights. You're now receiving unprompted thoughts or images that provide a sense of knowing what's next on your path to even more joy and abundance.

There's nothing you *have* to do. Just follow your heart and do what you're undeniably inspired to do. If anything doesn't feel just right, hold on a little longer until it does, or let it be okay to let it go if that's what feels best to you.

Let your focus be on anything that brings you joy and all that you want will unfold right before your eyes in the most delightful way.

Just keep telling your new story. The story of how you wish your life to be. Only it's not just a wish.

It's yours.
It's available to you.
It's time.
You're ready.
You have a strong desire for it.
You believe in it.
You're feeling it.
You're energetically aligned with it.
It's done.
All your wishes and dreams are coming true.

You are now mastering your alignment with all that you desire, and it can be no other way for you. And so it shall be.

We hope this book has helped you on your life's journey to feel even more empowered and limitless in your ability to create the life you wish for. If you're looking to further your journey of self-discovery, keep an eye out for more journals, workbooks, and courses. It's truly a great pleasure working with you!

Thank you so much...

I hope you enjoyed the book and will continue to benefit from having read it. If you're interested in being notified about upcoming courses, journals or workbooks, as well as any giveaways, please visit our website https://wishmorewellness.com/ and subscribe to the mailing list or follow my Amazon author page.

I would also appreciate it so much if you would **please consider doing a review of this book on Amazon.** It's very helpful to an author's success, and it would mean so much to me.

Thank you!

WHAT'S NEXT?

Don't forget to join the FREE Mini-Workshop (about 30-40 Minutes) where I share how I went from daily struggle to what feels like blissful wellbeing...

FREE MINI-WORKSHOP
3 Steps to Wellbeing & Achieving Your Dreams

Includes Guided Visualization Exercises
https://courses.wishmorewellness.com/courses/Mini-Workshop-3-Steps

More JOURNALS and a WORKBOOK SERIES...

Join my website mailing list at https://wishmorewellness.com/ or follow on Amazon
amazon.com/author/susanbalogh **to receive updates on new releases!**

PLEASE also share your success stories with me!
Be sure to join the Wish*More Wellness Facebook Group
so you can share any milestones or achievements that manifest for you,
or feel free to email me at suebalogh@wishmorewellness.com.
I would love to hear your stories, truly!

★★★

Share the Love & Gift a Friend!

Do you know someone who could use this book?

You can gift the Kindle version directly into their email inbox. Just choose the Amazon purchase option "Buy for Others."

★★★ The Wish*More Wellness Project ★★★

Be sure to join the Wish*More Wellness Facebook Group so you can help us grow a community of uplifters by sharing any milestones or achievements that manifest for you. Use the hashtag #wishmorewellness on social media when posting your thoughts, if desired. Or feel free to email me at suebalogh@wishmorewellness.com. I would absolutely love to hear your stories!

I invite you to preview my first book.
It's been called "life-changing," "enlightening," "magical," and "fun."

https://www.amazon.com/dp/B099PZC9T1

100 Days of Actions & Intentions to Create the Life You Wish For

"Imagine meeting a best friend each day, someone who always has your best interests at heart, someone who has great conversations that help you heal and flourish. This book is like having that best friend, day after day, being a loving companion helping you to heal and be well. I am going to use this book to help me make a lifetime habit of creating a life I desire, day after day after day."

~ Dr. Aloha Lavina, Managing Director of Arkipelago Consulting

"Oh, it had me at the front cover. I loved the bite-sized, the idea of reading a book one page/day at a time. If you like being interactive with your books and you like adding a touch of magic to your life, this book is ideal. A little cracker to forever keep on the shelf and you can do it as many times as you like."

~ Dr. Jennifer Meyer, meyersamuse.com

"Thought provoking and inspirational! This is a great little book that is very positive, upbeat and inspirational. It is written so that you can read it in short bursts made up of 100 small chapters."

~ Scott B. Allan, Bestselling author and top reviewer

"This book inspires to take action every day. From the powerful start with a "Promise to Myself" pledge, through action steps to take towards a renewed mindset, and intentional shaping of our own future and well being. Definitely a great way of starting the day and setting the stage for success."

~ Agi Kadar, FDN, CES, healthbalanced.com

Preview it here:
https://www.amazon.com/dp/B099PZC9T1

★ Also By Susan Balogh ★

BOOKS
100 Days of Actions & Intentions to Create the Life You Wish For
https://www.amazon.com/dp/B099PZC9T1

Dear Wellbeing: 100 Days on My Path to More Joy. A Self-Discovery Workbook
http://amzn.com/B08PCGR4JD

FREE MINI-WORKSHOP
3 Steps to Wellbeing & Achieving Your Dreams
https://courses.wishmorewellness.com/courses/Mini-Workshop-3-Steps

AUDIO-VIDEO COURSE
12-Week Holistic Healing & Happiness Course

ONLINE SERVICES
1:1 Coaching for Mindset/Happiness/Manifesting
Positive EFT Coaching (Meridian Tapping)
Energy Healing, Guided Meditation
Reiki I & II and Master/Teacher Certification
All or part available by video conference

Set Yourself Free & Be Happy!

All of the above are available at
http://wishmorewellness.com/services/
Find us on Instagram @Wishmore_Wellness
https://www.instagram.com/wishmore_wellness/
Please join the Wishmore Wellness FacebookGroup
https://www.facebook.com/groups/2061444523962316

About the Author

Susan Balogh is a holistic healing and happiness coach, author, and speaker who has a passion for helping others tap into their true power to achieve any state of mind that allows them to achieve their goals and dreams.

With a desire to heal herself and help others, Susan sought training for over 20 years in many healing modalities and learned how to turn pain and struggle into what she calls blissful wellbeing!

In her first book, *100 Days of Actions & Intentions to Create the Life You Wish For,* Susan loves to evoke every possible emotion from her readers to help them reach their full potential.

Susan is from Western New York, but travels the country in her custom (and very pink) RV to provide donation-based teaching. She had a vision of doing this for a couple years before leaving her 20-year hospital job. She also happens to love driving *anywhere* for *any* reason.

When she's not behind the wheel or writing or coaching, you might find her walking, biking, making jewelry, or spending time with family. She is a certified Reiki Master/Teacher, Qi Gong instructor, and happiness coach. More information about Susan and her offerings can be found at www.wishmorewellness.com.

Set Yourself Free & Be Happy!

You're perfect and exactly where you're meant to be in your life right now and constantly becoming more of who you truly are, and will always be moving toward a better place.

All good things come your way with effortless ease. The possibilities are limitless.

This is only the beginning, and you're moving forward and upward on your journey of life.

Let each kind word, thought, and action begin with you and create a better life for you and those around you, one moment at a time.

Wishing you more freedom, love & all that you wish for.

Susan

Wheresoever you go, go with all your heart – *Confucius*

Made in the USA
Monee, IL
10 November 2022

17507136R00079